gorgeousgreens

Annie Bell

gorgeousgreens

with photographs by Chris Alack

Kyle Cathie Ltd

First published in Great Britain in 2009 by
Kyle Cathie Limited
122 Arlington Road, London NW1 7HP
general.enquiries@kyle-cathie.com
www.kylecathie.com

978 1 85626 839 4

A CIP catalogue record for this title is available from the British Library.

10 9 8 7 6 5 4 3 2 1

Editor: Suzanna de Jong
Design: pinkstripedesign@hotmail.com
Copy Editor: Annie Lee
Proofreader: Stephanie Evans
Indexer: Ann Kingdom
Photographer: Chris Alack
Home Economist: Kim Morphew
Prop Stylist: Sue Radcliffe
Production: Sha Huxtable

Colour reproduction: Colourscan, Singapore
Printed and bound in Singapore by Star Standard Industries Pty Ltd

contents

introduction

The 'greens' of my childhood were a narrow concept: leafy cabbages that were normally boiled, with the leftovers turned into bubble and squeak, which was the best bit. We gobbled them up because we were told to, with almost every dinner at certain times of the year. But this is harking back to the Sixties and Seventies, long before all things green had become desirable, while today the term 'greens' is a fond one that has come to mean any vegetable, not just cabbage leaves, though these too have advanced beyond all recognition.

A large part of the advance has been to do with the way we cook. Looking back as recently as even ten years ago,

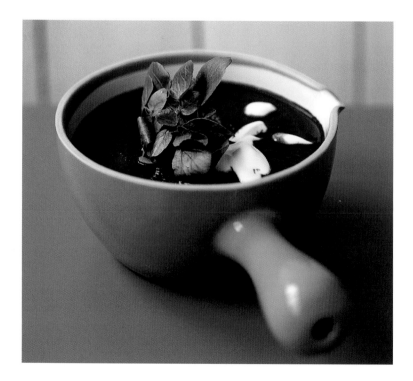

to when I first wrote a book on vegetables, pretty much the only roasted veg in it were parsnips and potatoes, and salads had yet to blossom into the big blowsy affairs we have become accustomed to seeing piled high in the windows of glam cafés. Where once they were a slap on the wrist after a few days' indulgence, today they are actually used to lure us in. I have a complete passion for green salads, hence an entire chapter is devoted to them. One of my favourite standby suppers revolves around roast chicken and small crispy potatoes, which leaves lots of time to spend whisking up a salad dressing and washing and drying a selection of green leaves, for wiping the plate clean of gravy. And there is little better way of rounding off any mealtime than with a sliver of goat's cheese or mature Cheddar and a pile of crisp, lightly dressed leaves.

But it's not all austerity – gratins possess the essential yummy factor, with their crisp edges and gooey cheese. And there is a chapter on 'green mains', filled with lovely tarts – miniature pizzettas made with puff pastry, deep, lightly set creamy quiches and hearty pies. I also experiment with grains more and more, like spelt and quinoa; with us since time immemorial, they have acquired a new lease of life. In fact, I suspect if we really wanted to predict the next grain fad, we need look no further than a pharaoh's tomb, since the fashion at the moment is for rediscovery.

The opening chapter of the book, however, is a rather more recent trip back in time, and one I personally find

nostalgic: a medley of dips. I adore dips, which were as central to my childhood as bubble and squeak, but ultimately they're as contemporary as what you dunk in them. As fridge raiding goes it doesn't get much healthier, and these make a great standby.

The chapter on potatoes spans all our favourite ways of serving them: lots of salads, sautéd, baked and stuffed, and little is more comforting than when they form the basis of a soup with a good chicken stock.

As well as the type of dish, the choice of vegetables is getting better and better. Some twenty years ago tomatoes were 'standard', perfectly round red fruits a little bigger than a plum, with nothing very thrilling to recommend either their appearance or their flavour. Whereas now, come summer, we are spoilt with cherry tomatoes in sunny shades of orange and red, some cocktail-sized and on the vine, baby plums and others little larger than a raisin. At the other end of the scale there are big beefsteak tomatoes dripping with juices, and wonderful heirloom varieties with amorphic shapes and pleated tops. With a little hunting we can amass a stunning collection of types to feast on.

Then there are greens themselves, which go so much further than boiling. The choice has been broadened out to include cavolo nero, a bubbly dark green leaf with a real depth of flavour, not dissimilar from our own derided kale, that takes on a new dimension when bought in the same fashion – on the stalk – and stripped off it. But my real new love is long-stem broccoli. While spring has long been a treat of a season for purple sprouting broccoli with its sweet flavour and tender stalks, we are now rarely without some variety of long-stem broccoli during the remainder of the year. It's at its best blanched, brushed with olive oil and griddled, which opens up the way for all manner of wonderful salads where it can be married with other gutsy ingredients like lentils and dates.

And next up is chicory, a vegetable we are just on the cusp of discovering, having long regarded the pale green *chicons* so appreciated in the Netherlands, Belgium and France as being strangely bitter. They are sublime tossed with olive oil and thrown into a hot oven, and make for delicious salads with sweet mustardy dressings. Any food with an edge, be it sour, salty, sweet or hot, can be married with foods offering the opposite. These leaves lap up blue cheese, salty bacon and hams, and sweet ingredients such as dried figs and prunes come to life. We seem at last to be taking the red varieties on board too.

Bringing all these lovely greens together, there is probably no more pivotal an arrival on these shores than extra virgin olive oil. Those poor pioneering spirits of the Fifties and earlier in following their heart to the Mediterranean were forced to rely on small bottles of olive oil (not even extra virgin) from the

chemist once they returned home, where it was normally sold for medicinal purposes. By the time I started cooking in the Eighties extra virgin olive oil was a given, and if I count the number of recipes in the book that rely on it, we are approaching some eighty per cent. I'm not sure where greens would be today in its absence.

Even though this book isn't strictly vegetarian, any meat or fish is incidental, and if you are someone who normally eschews them you will still find plenty to please. The recipes are more than anything a celebration of the produce itself. Farmers' markets and specialised shops are glorious hunting grounds for really good veggies – big boxes piled high with soil-crusted roots, cabbages with snails clinging inside their outer leaves, carrots and beetroot with their tops attached, a general sense of things having only recently been pulled from a field, casting in their turn a general sense of well-being that comes with eating lots of gorgeous greens.

dips

For those of us who can remember the Seventies, dips will be forever entwined with full-length orange check evening dresses. They're very In The Lounge with Andy Williams. In fact, one of my earliest memories of party time as a child was of my mother's 'dip', a triumph of its time. A couple of packets of Philly whizzed in a blender with a little chopped onion or shallot, a squeeze of lemon juice and enough milk to give it a dipping consistency, liberally dusted with cayenne pepper. 'Crisps and Dip' were fantastically good and just as bad for you – the calories don't bear thinking about.

Several decades down the line, judging from chill cabinets, we still can't get enough, though inevitably they have evolved, or rather the dunkers have. Scooped straight from the tub with some cherry tomatoes or slivers of carrot, dips today are one of the healthiest of snacks and will lure the most reluctant veg-o-phobe, in the same way that a little melted chocolate will convince the fruit-shy to eat up their apples.

Crudités tend to taste better the thinner you cut them; hard and crisp with a little bite soothed by a big dollop of a creamy dip seems to cut the right balance. And younger veg fare better than old – baby fennel bulbs, slender young carrots and celery hearts. Or look to the Lebanese, who make a fine art of raw vegetables at the start of every meal. A plate of peppers, tomatoes, spring onions, baby cucumbers, a half lettuce and some radishes will arrive with beads of water clinging, and with it a selection of pickles.

Dust dips with a little crushed cumin or toasted coriander seed and give them a drizzle of oil, and they are at the ready for a more elegant selection of eats. You can play on the Greek mezze inherent in them by serving a couple of dips with marinated olives, a block of feta to chip away at, and some warm pitta breads cooked on a griddle until they're branded with a golden lattice pattern.

This is something like a baba ghanoush, without the raw rasp of garlic it normally carries in its wake. Pomegranate offsets the faint bitterness of the aubergines, as do the toasted almonds, and it's altogether gentler.

aubergine purée with pomegranate and almonds

1kg aubergines (3 large ones)
4 slices of day-old white bread,
   crusts removed, torn into pieces
1 garlic clove, peeled and
   coarsely chopped
1 tablespoon red wine vinegar
5 tablespoons extra virgin olive oil,
   plus extra to serve
sea salt, black pepper
1 tablespoon lemon juice
seeds from ½ pomegranate
1 tablespoon toasted flaked almonds

Serves 6

Preheat the oven to 200°C fan/220°C/gas mark 7. Prick the aubergines all over and bake for 25 minutes, until the skin is wrinkled and darker. While they are cooking, soak the bread in water for 5 minutes, then squeeze out the water, though it shouldn't be too dry. Place the bread in a food processor with the garlic and vinegar and process to a smooth cream. With the motor running, add the olive oil.

Skin the aubergines and thickly slice the cooked flesh. Place it in a sieve and press out as much juice as possible. Add the flesh to the bread mixture in the food processor and purée together, adding some seasoning. Transfer the purée to a shallow bowl. You can prepare the recipe to this point in advance.

To serve, drizzle a swirl of oil and the lemon juice on top of the purée. Scatter the pomegranate seeds and flaked almonds over.

These could just as well be served alone as together, but they do complement each other especially well, trailing the Provençal Riviera in their wake. You can serve any mixture of crudités – fine slivers of celery heart, red and yellow cherry tomatoes and strips of pepper. Radishes too: try to buy these by the bunch, as their foliage is the best indicator of their freshness. Long, slim breakfast radishes are the tastiest of all.

crushed goat's cheese and anchoïade

Crushed Goat's Cheese

225g medium-mature goat's cheese, e.g.
   Crottin de Chavignol, rind removed
3 tablespoons extra virgin olive oil
black pepper
a few slivers of spring onion,
   white and green parts

Anchoïade

4 garlic cloves, peeled
16 anchovy fillets in oil
15 green olives, pitted
150ml extra virgin olive oil
1 teaspoon sherry vinegar

Serves 6

To make the crushed goat's cheese, crumble the cheese into a bowl and mash to a coarse paste with the olive oil and black pepper. Serve in a small bowl with a few fine slivers of spring onion scattered over.

To make the anchoïade, place the garlic, anchovies and olives in a food processor and reduce to a coarse purée. Add the olive oil and vinegar and process at high speed until you have a smooth paste.

As the season for broad beans progresses their skins toughen and the flesh becomes that much more mealy, and here the purée is sieved, making it a good one for midsummer. But equally it's a real quickie should you have a packet of frozen broad beans hanging around the freezer. Some cooked tail-on prawns and quail's eggs would make delicious dunkers, as do warm pitta breads. Alternatively you could spoon it on top of crisp fried sea bream or sea bass fillets by way of a sauce.

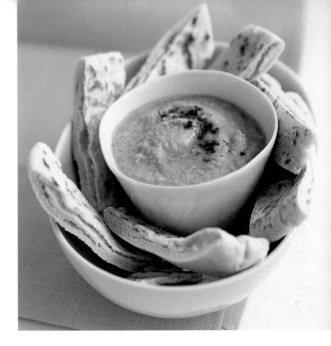

spicy broad bean dip

700g fresh or frozen broad beans

¾ teaspoon chopped medium hot green chilli

1 level teaspoon ground cumin

1 teaspoon paprika, plus extra for dusting

1 garlic clove, peeled and chopped

sea salt, black pepper

7 tablespoons extra virgin olive oil, plus extra to serve

juice of 1 lemon

Serves 6

Cook the broad beans in boiling water for 8 minutes if fresh, 3–4 minutes if frozen. Purée them in a food processor with the chilli, cumin, paprika, garlic and some seasoning, trickling in the olive oil and lemon juice. Pass through a sieve into a bowl and serve drizzled with olive oil and sprinkled with paprika.

This sweet and moreish dip may find fans among you for its absence of garlic and raw onion, though more to the point it is low-fat. I'd think in terms of a little salad of grated courgette and some caper berries alongside, or a few slices of salami rolled up and skewered with a cocktail stick, as well as some crackers or bread.

red pepper mezze

6 red peppers

1 slice of coarse-textured white
  bread, toasted

75g pine nuts, toasted

2 tablespoons Greek yoghurt

a squeeze of lemon juice

sea salt, black pepper

1 tablespoon each of chopped
  fresh coriander and mint, plus extra
  to serve

Serves 6–8

Roast the peppers for 20 minutes at 200°C fan/220°C/gas mark 7, then place them in a bowl, cover and leave to cool. Reduce the toast to crumbs in a food processor, then whiz the pine nuts to coarse nibs. Skin and deseed the peppers and purée in the food processor.

Transfer the purée to a bowl and stir in the breadcrumbs, pine nuts, yoghurt, lemon juice, some seasoning and the herbs. Leave to stand for an hour or so before eating, and serve with a few extra herbs scattered over.

This dip plays on the better nature of pumpkins and butternut squash to reduce to a silken purée; they also lap up spices and other aromatics, which makes them a great medium for all things Middle Eastern. Olives and a sharp sheep's cheese go down well here too.

pumpkin dip

600g butternut squash
  or pumpkin flesh
juice of 1 lemon
6 tablespoons extra virgin olive oil,
  plus extra to serve
1 teaspoon harissa
1 garlic clove, peeled and crushed
  to a paste
1 teaspoon ground coriander
sea salt, black pepper
coarsely chopped fresh coriander
  (optional)

Serves 6

Steam the squash or pumpkin flesh for 15 minutes until tender. Transfer to a bowl and coarsely mash, then combine with the lemon juice, olive oil, harissa, garlic, ground coriander, sea salt and black pepper. Transfer to a clean bowl, drizzle with a little more olive oil and scatter with chopped coriander if wished.

Dyed a sunny yellow courtesy of a pinch of saffron, this is that little bit more thrilling than ordinary tzatziki, which we have on tap in any case – ready-made tubs are one of the healthiest dips in the chill cabinet.

saffron tzatziki

a pinch of saffron filaments
  (approx. 20)
1 tablespoon extra virgin olive oil,
  plus a little extra to serve
1 teaspoon white wine vinegar
225g Greek yoghurt
½ teaspoon caster sugar
sea salt
½ cucumber
1 heaped teaspoon finely chopped
  shallot
1 heaped teaspoon finely sliced mint,
  plus a little extra to serve
cayenne pepper

Serves 4

Grind the saffron in a pestle and mortar and infuse in a teaspoon of boiling water for 15 minutes. Whisk the olive oil, vinegar, yoghurt, saffron infusion, sugar and a little salt together in a bowl. Peel the cucumber, quarter lengthways, remove the seeds and dice the flesh very finely by first slicing the quarters into thin strips. Add the cucumber, shallot and mint to the bowl, and taste for seasoning. To serve, decorate with a swirl of olive oil, a little finely sliced mint and a dusting of cayenne pepper.

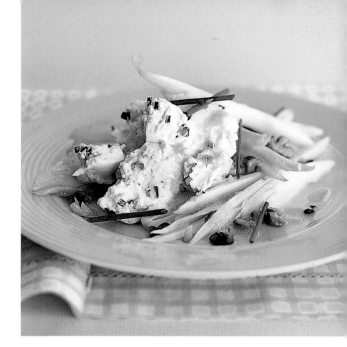

With its Norman roots this dip has subtly changing textures, and relies on an aromatic mature goat's cheese with a dash of Calvados to bring out its character. You want something that's slightly runny at the edges while chalky within. A simpler aside to the salad that lends itself to being a little starter or light lunch would be chicory leaves and halved walnuts, and thick slices of pain de Campagne or sourdough bread.

creamy goat's cheese

Creamy Goat's Cheese

150g young fresh goat's cheese

200g mature goat's cheese, rind removed

50g crème fraîche

3 teaspoons cider vinegar

1 tablespoon Calvados or brandy

½ garlic clove, crushed to a paste

1 tablespoon finely chopped fresh chives,
   plus a few extra to serve

Salad

1 level teaspoon Dijon mustard

sea salt, black pepper

1 tablespoon walnut oil

1 tablespoon groundnut oil

2 heads of chicory, base trimmed

25g walnuts, finely chopped

Serves 4

Mash the goat's cheeses and the crème fraîche together in a bowl to a textured cream. Blend 1 teaspoon of the vinegar, the Calvados and crushed garlic into the goat's cheese, and stir in the chives. Transfer it to a clean bowl, cover and chill until required. The recipe can be prepared to this point in advance.

Make the salad as close to the time of eating as possible to avoid the chicory discolouring. Whisk the remaining vinegar with the mustard and some seasoning in a bowl, then whisk in the oils until the dressing is thick and creamy. Discard the outer chicory leaves, halve the heads lengthways and cut out the central core. Finely slice the leaves into long strips and toss with the dressing in a bowl, then mix in the walnuts. Serve the salad with a large dollop of creamed goat's cheese and a few chives scattered over.

An excellent use for the last of a big hunk of Stilton, which makes it a good one around Christmas; the slightly dry cheese towards the rind that gets left until the end is just as tasty as the centre, if not so appetising to behold. I first encountered sherried Stilton as a tapa in Seville, which may provide some inspiration for how to eat it other than with this crisp little salad – it's heaven with little warm crusty white rolls and a small glass of fino.

sherried stilton

Sherried Stilton
300g Stilton (weight excluding rind)
4 tablespoons medium sherry

Salad
500g cooked and peeled beetroot
  (unvinegared), cut into slim wedges
2 tablespoons extra virgin olive oil
2 teaspoons sherry vinegar
2 teaspoons lemon juice
sea salt, black pepper
pale green celery leaves from 2 heads,
  sliced lengthways if large
50g pecan nuts, thinly sliced
wafer-thin toast soldiers to serve

Serves 6

Coarsely crumble the Stilton into a bowl. Pour over the sherry and gently mash to a textured purée.

To make the salad, toss the beetroot with the oil, vinegar, lemon juice and some seasoning in a bowl, then mix in three-quarters of the celery leaves and nuts. Divide the salad between six side plates and scatter the remaining celery leaves and nuts over. Place 1 tablespoon of the cheese to the side and serve with toast soldiers.

Alternatively place the salad in a salad bowl, and the cheese in another bowl, and leave everyone to help themselves.

Harry's Bar refer to this as a pâté, but as it has a dippy kind of consistency it's game for slivers of nascent vegetables and shards of toasted flat-bread, as well as being yummy dolloped on to toast. It's a particularly useful one, given how many of us have a couple of tins of tuna sitting at the back of the cupboard, and it's comforting to know you can whiz up a halfway glamorous offering at the drop of a hat.

harry's bar tuna dip

2 x 200g tins of tuna in brine,
  well drained
1 tablespoon lemon juice
1 tablespoon brandy
sea salt, black pepper
3 tablespoons mayonnaise
cayenne pepper
grissini, radishes and caper
  berries to serve

Serves 6

Whiz the tuna in a food processor with the lemon juice, brandy and some seasoning. Transfer the fish to a bowl and beat in the mayonnaise. Serve dusted with cayenne pepper, accompanied by grissini, radishes and caper berries.

roasted veg

The word 'roasted' here is more of a description of the end result than the means of getting there. Whether you show them a hot oven, a griddle or a frying pan, vegetables that emerge silken, patched with gold and soaked in olive oil have an appetising allure that makes boiling seem like a dull cousin. And they have revolutionised our eating habits. In fact it's hard to believe that until some fifteen years ago roasted potatoes and parsnips were about as far as it went.

Roasted veg go hand in hand with all things Mediterranean, though there is no need for them to be confined to the summer art of roasted peppers, courgettes and aubergines and their attendant maidens, olives, Parmesan and anchovies, tempting as these are. Winter is equally good, and there are very few roots that don't respond to a little Italianate flair when cooked with olive oil, whole garlic cloves and woody resinous herbs. Slim carrots shorn of their tops, beetroots in their skins, chunks of celeriac, floppy flat-cap mushrooms, quarters of onion, spears of long-stem broccoli and even chicory are just as adept at emerging crisp and singed at the fringes. They're masters of delusion, too: something that has been roasted, even if eaten cold, leaves you feeling warmed and as though you've had a 'proper' dinner.

Vegetables cooked in this fashion have become one of the great basics of the kitchen. And most of the recipes here are suggestions for ways of dressing them up, but you could just as easily deconstruct the ideas to give you the basics for apéritif grazing, or for popping into a sandwich or eating on toast. They may also inspire a soup, or a salad with some peppery cresses and pulses. Basically they're building blocks.

This is a really vibrant tomato soup that is so much richer in flavour for the tomatoes having been roasted in a very hot oven. As well as serving it steaming hot, like gazpacho it's perfect supped ice-cool on a very hot day. If you want to pan it out, it's delicious dished up with youngish goat's cheeses steeped in olive oil with lemon zest, garlic and thyme. Also a little salad of slivers of fennel and orange, black olives and parsley wouldn't go amiss.

roasted tomato and basil soup

1.5kg tomatoes on the vine
extra virgin olive oil
sea salt, black pepper
½ teaspoon caster sugar
about 8 large fresh basil leaves,
    plus a few tinies to serve

Serves 4

Preheat the oven to 220°C fan/240°C/gas mark 9. Arrange the tomatoes in a large roasting dish in a single layer, drizzle over 3 tablespoons of oil and roast for 20 minutes.

Once they are cool enough to handle, pinch the tomatoes off the vines using a fork, and tip into a liquidiser with the roasting juices. Add a good dose of salt, some black pepper, the sugar, the basil leaves and another 3 tablespoons of oil, and liquidise. Pass through a sieve, then gently reheat in a saucepan. Serve each bowl with a drizzle of oil and a couple of small basil leaves in the centre.

I love the sheer simplicity of this Barbara Cartland pink soup, it's true to the vegetable. While boiled beetroot can be insipid and unfriendly, and to me recalls Russian state-run hotels back in the days when the red flag was flying, roasting them concentrates their flavour and brings out their sweetness, as does a little lemon.

roast beetroot and lemon soup with watercress

1kg good-sized raw beetroot
3 tablespoons extra virgin olive oil
sea salt, black pepper
1 strip of lemon zest, removed with a
    potato peeler, and 1 tablespoon
    lemon juice
crème fraîche and coarsely chopped
    watercress, or a sprig, to serve

Serves 4

Preheat the oven to 220°C fan/240°C/gas mark 9. Without peeling the beetroot, trim the tops and bottoms of shoots and roots, and quarter or cut into wedges. Arrange these in a large roasting dish, pour over the olive oil, season and roast for 40 minutes until tender, stirring halfway through.

Liquidise the contents of the roasting pan in batches with 800ml of water, the lemon zest and juice, and plenty of seasoning. Pass through a sieve into a saucepan and gently reheat. Serve with a spoonful of crème fraîche and lots of chopped watercress, or a sprig.

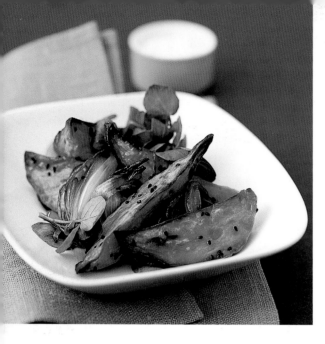

Dished up while the potatoes and onions are still warm, the horseradish sauce languidly melts over the top.

roast sweet potatoes with horseradish

1.2kg small orange-fleshed sweet
   potatoes, peeled and quartered
   lengthways, halved if long
extra virgin olive oil
1 level tablespoon onion seeds
sea salt, black pepper
2 large red onions, peeled, halved and
   thinly sliced
2 tablespoons finely grated fresh
   horseradish, or 2 teaspoons
   prepared sauce
150g crème fraîche
watercress to serve 4

Serves 4

Preheat the oven to 220°C fan/240°C/gas mark 9. Toss the sweet potatoes in a large bowl with 3 tablespoons of olive oil, the onion seeds and some seasoning, then tip into a large roasting dish that will hold them in a crowded single layer and roast for 30–40 minutes, stirring halfway through. At the same time, toss the onions in a large bowl with a couple of tablespoons of oil, then spread these out on a baking sheet and roast for 15–17 minutes, until golden and caramelised, stirring halfway through. Blend the horseradish with the crème fraîche and a little salt.

Mix the onions into the sweet potatoes. Toss the watercress with 1 tablespoon of olive oil and a little salt. Serve the potatoes with the horseradish spooned on top, and a pile of watercress. The veg are just as good eaten cold, in which case forego the sauce.

This is a great way of roasting red onions. They turn out crispy at the edges and intensely sweet, and they're gorgeous scattered over pretty much any salad or stuffed into a sarnie with some rare roast beef or a chicken kebab.

salad of beetroot, roasted red onions and rocket

700g red onions, peeled, halved and thickly sliced

6 tablespoons extra virgin olive oil

2 teaspoons fresh thyme leaves

sea salt, black pepper

1 teaspoon balsamic vinegar

50g skinned hazelnuts

500g cooked and peeled beetroot (unvinegared), halved and cut into wedges

3 tablespoons coarsely snipped fresh chives

a handful of rocket leaves

Serves 6

Preheat the oven to 180°C fan/200°C/gas mark 6. Scatter the onion slices over the base of a roasting dish in a crowded single layer and drizzle over 4 tablespoons of olive oil. Scatter over the thyme and a little salt, and roast for 40–45 minutes until golden, stirring halfway through. Drizzle over the vinegar and leave to cool. At the same time as roasting the onions, scatter the hazelnuts over the base of a small baking dish, toast in the oven for 10 minutes until golden, then remove and leave to cool.

Toss the beetroot, onion and hazelnuts in a large salad bowl with another couple of tablespoons of oil and season. Mix in the chives and rocket leaves.

Pasta quills and shavings of Parmesan are also particularly fine with roasted butternut, in which case a dash of balsamic vinegar will do you in lieu of the harissa.

roasted squash and lentils with harissa dressing

2 butternut squash (approx. 800g each)
7 tablespoons extra virgin olive oil
sea salt, black pepper
200g French green lentils
2 large red onions, peeled, halved and
  thinly sliced
130g lamb's lettuce

Dressing
2 teaspoons harissa
2 teaspoons lemon juice
2 tablespoons extra virgin olive oil

Serves 4–6

Heat the oven to 190°C fan/210°C/gas mark 6. Slice the top and bottom off the squash, then halve them and cut off the skin. Quarter the bulbs to remove the seeds and slice these sections into wedges. Halve the remaining cylindrical trunks lengthways and slice 1cm thick. Arrange the squash in a roasting dish in a crowded single layer – I use one 38 x 25cm. Drizzle over 3 tablespoons of olive oil, season and roast for 1 hour. Turn the squash after 30 minutes, and again after 45 minutes.

About 20 minutes after putting the squash in to roast, bring a medium-sized pan of water to the boil. Add the lentils and cook for about 25 minutes until just tender, then drain into a sieve.

Toss the onions with 2 tablespoons of oil, scatter over the base of a large roasting dish, and put into the oven when the squash have been cooking for 35 minutes to cook for the rest of the time. Stir them halfway through.

Add the onions and lentils to the pan with the squash and pour over the remaining oil. Scatter over some salt and gently turn, using a spatula.

Whisk the harissa and lemon juice together in a bowl, then whisk in the oil. Pour this over the salad leaves in a bowl, and serve the salad piled on top of the squash and lentils. The squash and lentils can also be served at room temperature, in which case dress the salad at the last minute.

two ways with mushrooms

Divine as Portabello mushrooms are, here you want the bog-standard flat-cap ones that are that little bit deeper.

grilled manchego-stuffed mushrooms

90g sourdough or other
   open-textured white bread
   (weight excluding crusts)
12 flat-cap mushrooms, stalks
   trimmed level with caps
8 tablespoons extra virgin olive oil

sea salt, black pepper
12 thin triangles of Manchego
   (approx. 130g excluding rind)
12 fresh sage leaves

Serves 6

Preheat the oven to 200°C fan/220°C/gas mark 7. Break up the bread and whiz to coarse crumbs in a food processor. Arrange the mushrooms in 2 roasting dishes. Drizzle over 3 tablespoons of oil and season them. Lay one Manchego slice in the centre of each mushroom, breaking off the tip if necessary so it lies within the edges of the mushroom. Place a sage leaf on top, then drizzle over another 3 tablespoons of oil. Toss the breadcrumbs with the remaining 2 tablespoons of oil and scatter over. Bake for 15 minutes, until the cheese is crusty and golden at the edges and the breadcrumbs are toasted and crisp.

The ham wrapped around the mushrooms turns to a papery crisp in the oven, sealing in the moussey goat's cheese and all those satanically dark mushroom juices.

portabello mushrooms wrapped in prosciutto with goat's cheese

8 Portabello mushrooms
extra virgin olive oil
sea salt, black pepper
225g chèvre log, rind
   removed, sliced
8 slices of prosciutto

Serves 4

Preheat the oven to 180°C fan/200°C/gas mark 6. Cut the stalks off the mushrooms level with the caps. Brush the mushrooms on both sides with olive oil and season them. Divide the goat's cheese between the caps and wrap each mushroom in a slice of prosciutto, placing it over the mushroom cap and tucking the pieces underneath. Arrange the mushrooms in a roasting dish cup side up, drizzle over a couple of tablespoons of oil and bake for 25 minutes, until the prosciutto has begun to crisp up and the cheese is melted and golden at the edges.

It is increasingly easy to get hold of yellow or golden beetroot, which have an excellent flavour and cook up in exactly the same fashion as purple ones, and they make a fine change. You could also stir in some chopped leafy herbs – flat-leaf parsley, chives or chervil – here.

grilled broccoli and beetroot with lentils

700g small uncooked beetroot

4 small sprigs of fresh rosemary

extra virgin olive oil

juice of 1½ lemons

3 garlic cloves, peeled and crushed
  to a paste

sea salt, black pepper

250g French green lentils

400g purple sprouting or tenderstem
  broccoli, trimmed

Serves 6

Preheat the oven to 220°C fan/240°C/gas mark 9. Trim the shoots of the beetroots to within 1cm of the top, but leave the whiskery tail intact, and give them a good scrub. Place them in a large bowl. Pull off half the rosemary needles and scatter these and the twigs over the beetroots. Toss with 4 tablespoons of olive oil, the juice of 1 lemon, the garlic, and some seasoning. Tip into a roasting dish and roast for 30–40 minutes, until the skins are golden and puffy and the insides tender, turning them halfway through. Leave to stand for about 10 minutes.

At the same time as roasting the beetroot, bring a large pan of water to the boil. Add the lentils and cook for 20–25 minutes until tender, then drain them into a sieve. Bring another pan of water to the boil, add the broccoli and cook for 3 minutes, then drain and leave for a few minutes for the surface moisture to evaporate. Heat a ridged griddle over a medium heat. Toss the broccoli in a large bowl with a couple of tablespoons of oil and some seasoning, and grill in two or three batches for 2–3 minutes each side until golden.

Trim the top and bottom of the beetroots, and quarter or slice into wedges. Place them in a large shallow serving dish and scatter the lentils over. Pour over the roasting oil with another 4 tablespoons of oil, the remaining lemon juice and some seasoning, and gently toss. Mix in the broccoli. This is delicious at any temperature, but if serving it cold you may need to add a little more oil.

This way of roasting peppers is a wardrobe basic – mix in some olives or slivers of anchovy and throw over some chopped parsley or egg. The layering gives the salad another dimension, with the practicality that you can assemble the whole caboodle well in advance of eating.

roasted pepper, rocket and parmesan salad

4 red or orange peppers, core,
   seeds and membranes removed
4–5 sprigs of fresh thyme
2 bay leaves
3 garlic cloves, peeled and sliced
6 tablespoons extra virgin olive oil
sea salt, black pepper
1 tablespoon balsamic vinegar
groundnut oil for shallow frying
2 large slices of white bread, 1cm
   thick, crusts removed, diced
100g thinly sliced Parmesan
100g rocket (preferably wild)

Serves 4

Preheat the oven to 180°C fan/200°C/gas mark 6. Cut each pepper into 8 long strips and arrange in a crowded single layer in a roasting dish. Tuck in the herbs and scatter over the garlic. Drizzle over 2 tablespoons of the olive oil and season. Roast for 45–50 minutes, stirring and basting at least twice to ensure the peppers emerge succulent and evenly singed at the edges. When they come out of the oven, drip over the vinegar, vaguely stir to mix it into the juices, and pour over the remaining 4 tablespoons of olive oil. Leave to cool.

In the meantime, heat about 7mm of groundnut oil in a large frying pan over a medium heat until hot enough to immerse a cube of bread in bubbles. Add the bread cubes and fry, turning frequently, until evenly gold and crisp. Remove them using a slotted spoon and drain on a double thickness of kitchen paper. Leave to cool.

Transfer the peppers and juices to a large, deep salad bowl. Arrange the Parmesan on top, then the rocket, and finally scatter over the croutons. Cover with clingfilm and set aside in a cool place. Just before eating, gently toss the salad ingredients together using two salad servers.

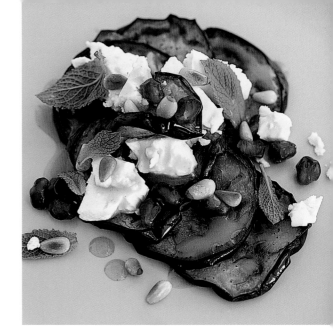

A lusciously thick honey sauce, the consistency of mayonnaise, that combined with feta and pine nuts whisks us off somewhere in the vicinity of Crete.

aubergines in honey

2 aubergines, stalk ends discarded,
    thickly sliced (about 1cm)
extra virgin olive oil
sea salt, black pepper
30g pine nuts
1 teaspoon Dijon mustard
2 teaspoons runny honey (ideally dark)
4 tablespoons groundnut or
    vegetable oil
a squeeze of lemon juice
150g feta, crumbled
seeds of ½ pomegranate
a handful of small fresh mint leaves

Serves 6

Heat a large non-stick frying pan over a medium heat (or you could use two). Take as many aubergine slices as will fit into the pan, brush them on one side with olive oil, season, and fry this side for 4–6 minutes, until golden. Brush the top side with oil, turn the slices over and fry this side for 3–4 minutes. Transfer the slices to a large plate and cook the remainder likewise. Leave the aubergine to cool.

At the same time, preheat the oven to 180°C fan/200°C/gas mark 6, spread the pine nuts out in a thin layer in a small baking dish and toast them for 8–10 minutes until lightly golden.

To prepare the sauce, whisk the mustard and honey together in a small bowl, and gradually whisk in the groundnut oil until you have a thick emulsion. Whisk in a squeeze of lemon juice until the sauce has a thick trickling consistency. You can prepare the recipe to this point in advance.

Arrange the aubergines either on a couple of large plates for handing round, or on 6 individual ones. Drizzle the sauce over the aubergines, scatter over the feta, pomegranate seeds, pine nuts and mint, and serve.

What could be nicer than breadcrumbs infused with garlic and anchovies stuffed inside red peppers? These are great as part of a Mediterranean mixed spread, and have a real hot-weather vibe to them, by which you can read relaxed.

anchovy-stuffed peppers

4 red or yellow peppers, or a mixture

sea salt, black pepper

extra virgin olive oil

5 garlic cloves, peeled and finely
   chopped

2 tablespoons fresh thyme leaves

15 salted anchovies, chopped

a knife tip of finely chopped dried chilli

200g fresh white breadcrumbs

Serves 4

Preheat the oven to 180°C fan/200°C/gas mark 6. Halve the peppers, keeping the stalks intact, and remove the seeds and membranes. Arrange the peppers cut side up in a roasting tray and season them inside with salt and pepper.

Heat a couple of tablespoons of olive oil in a large frying pan over a medium heat, add the garlic and briefly fry until aromatic and starting to colour. Stir in the thyme, anchovies and chilli, then the breadcrumbs. Remove from the heat and mix in another 5 tablespoons of olive oil. Use the mixture to loosely stuff the peppers, then drizzle a little more olive oil over and roast for 40–45 minutes, until the crumbs are golden and crisp. Leave to cool to room temperature.

The best sun-dried tomatoes are only semi-dry, and have the succulence of fresh tomatoes with the intensity of dried. These slow-roasted candy-sweet tomato petals are exquisite eaten with a tart goat's cheese and thick slices of toasted French bread drizzled with olive oil.

slow-roast tomatoes

1.5kg medium tomatoes
4 unpeeled garlic cloves, crushed
5 sprigs of fresh thyme
sea salt
caster sugar
extra virgin olive oil
a handful of fresh basil leaves

Serves 8

Preheat the oven to 120°C fan/140°C/gas mark 1. Bring a large pan of water to the boil. Cut out a cone from the top of each tomato to remove the core and plunge them first into the boiling water for 20 seconds and then into cold water. Remove them and slip off the skins, then halve and deseed them. Lay the tomato petals, cut side down, on a non-stick baking tray, scatter over the garlic and thyme and season with salt and a sprinkling of sugar. Drizzle over 4 tablespoons of olive oil and bake for 2 hours.

Once they are cool place them in a bowl or jar interspersed with the basil leaves, and cover with olive oil. If not serving straight away, cover and chill for up to three days, bringing back up to room temperature before serving.

This famous Turkish dish is so-called because the Imam fainted with pleasure either on eating it or at the shock at the amount of oil used to cook it. Traditionally the aubergines are braised, while here they are roasted. You could also throw some pitted black olives over the aubergines when you serve them.

imam bayildi

2 aubergines
extra virgin olive oil
sea salt, black pepper
2 beefsteak tomatoes
  (approx. 250g each)
1 large onion, peeled, halved
  and sliced
5 garlic cloves, peeled
  and finely chopped
3 tablespoons each coarsely chopped
  fresh flat-leaf parsley, dill and basil

Serves 4

Preheat the oven to 180°C fan/200°C/gas mark 6 and heat a ridged griddle over a medium heat for several minutes. Trim the stalk ends of the aubergines and halve them lengthways. Brush them all over with oil and season. Grill the cut surface for about 5 minutes until golden, then lay the aubergine halves cut side up in a baking dish. You will probably need to grill them in two batches.

In the meantime, bring a small pan of water to the boil and cut out a cone to remove the core from each tomato. Plunge them into the boiling water for about 20 seconds and then into cold water. Slip off their skins and coarsely chop them. Combine them in a bowl with the onion, garlic and herbs, add some seasoning and 6 tablespoons of olive oil, and toss.

Pile the vegetable mixture on top of the aubergines and roast for 40–45 minutes, until the vegetables are nicely golden. Leave to cool for at least 15 minutes, and serve either warm or at room temperature, with more olive oil poured over.

Courgettes change character completely when they are grilled – it's hard to believe they are the same vegetable as when eaten raw. This very simple means of cooking strips on a ridged griddle brings out their sweet aromatic succulence with the minimum of fuss.

char-grilled courgettes with pine nuts

50g pine nuts
4 medium courgettes, trimmed and
   sliced lengthways into strips
   0.5cm thick
extra virgin olive oil
sea salt, black pepper

Serves 6

Heat a dry frying pan over a medium heat and toast the pine nuts, stirring constantly until they are golden and fragrant.

Heat a ridged griddle over a medium heat. Lay some of the courgette slices out on a board, brush one side with olive oil, season, and grill oiled side down until striped. Brush the top side with oil (but don't season it), then turn and cook this side too. Repeat with the remaining courgette slices, removing them to a container as they are cooked. Splash over some olive oil, cover and leave in a cool place. Stir in the pine nuts shortly before serving

gratins

Gratins are the yummy factor in all things green, big comforting pies with crusty edges concealing meltingly tender vegetables within. They are the antithesis of lightly steamed veg with a dab of butter, there is no holding back on the olive oil or cream, and most are a play on our love of toasted cheese.

Little spreads comfort like the silken elasticity of a warm skein of mozzarella or a bubbling mass of Cheddar. The likes of Gorgonzola and Roquefort melt down to a salty river. Goat's cheeses in the mould of Crottins de Chavignol are rendered mousse-like and fluffy, while the mountain greats like Gruyère, Emmental and Raclette lead the way to fonduesque nirvana.

The most austere of vegetables invite us into a nostalgic comfort zone when cooked as gratins. The silken texture of greens such as spinach fuse seamlessly with molten cheese, while the normally dour sprout is reborn as a vamp when roasted with Dolcelatte. Slices of ripe tomato baked with lily-white goat's cheese exude a gorgeous pool of juices at the ready for a pile of toast.

Potatoes, however, are in a league of their own, in fact no need for cheese at all with that prized crispy top layer to share out. And if you are looking for something lighter, then the potato gratins tick all the alluring boxes without being unduly rich. Tossed with just a little olive oil, you can tuck into them with a big green salad and together they make a pretty virtuous line-up. The root vegetable and Cheddar gratin too is deceptively healthy, tasting a great deal more indulgent than it really is.

Soft skeins of molten mozzarella straight from the oven with an inky dark green mass of spinach is heartstoppingly good. But like any other fonduesque dish it does require diners to be at the ready the moment it emerges, to capture it at its best. A lightly poached egg would also be divine here, veering in the direction of eggs Florentine.

spinach and mozzarella gratin

extra virgin olive oil

2 red onions, peeled, halved
  and finely sliced

2 garlic cloves, peeled and
  finely chopped

sea salt, black pepper

1.2kg spinach

350g buffalo mozzarella (drained
  weight), sliced

200g baby plum tomatoes, halved

3 tablespoons oregano or
  marjoram leaves

thick slices of olive or sourdough
  bread, toasted and drizzled with
  olive oil, to serve

Serves 6

Heat a couple of tablespoons of oil in a large frying pan over a medium heat. Add the onions and fry for 8–10 minutes, stirring frequently, until silky and golden, adding the garlic and some seasoning just before the end, then transfer them to a bowl. You will need to cook the spinach in batches. Heat another tablespoon of oil in the frying pan, add a large pile of spinach and fry, tossing constantly until it wilts. Transfer it to a bowl and cook the remainder in the same fashion. Leave to cool.

Preheat the oven to 190°C fan/210°C/gas mark 6. Tip the spinach into a colander and press out the excess water using a potato masher. Lay half the leaves over the base of a 30cm oval gratin dish or one of equivalent size, season, then lay over half the onions and half the mozzarella and repeat. Scatter the tomatoes and oregano over the top. (You can prepare the gratin to this point in advance, in which case cover and chill.) Season, drizzle over another couple of tablespoons of oil and bake for 25–30 minutes, until the cheese is golden and sizzling. Serve immediately, with thick slices of toast drizzled with olive oil.

Brussels sprouts and cabbages are never so good as when they turn golden and crispy at the tips. With lashings of blue cheese, this would be yummy served with a seared steak or roast beef, though dedicated vegophiles will be happy to dive in there on its own and call it supper.

gratin of greens

1½ Sweetheart or pointed cabbages,
   base trimmed, outer leaves discarded
500g Brussels sprouts, base trimmed,
   outer leaves discarded and
   halved downwards
1 red onion, peeled, halved
   and thinly sliced
3 tablespoons extra virgin olive oil
sea salt, black pepper
200g Dolcelatte, diced

Serves 4

Bring a large pan of salted water to the boil. Cut the Sweetheart cabbage into thin wedges, leaving them attached by the thick central stalk at the base. Add the cabbage and sprouts to the pan and bring back to the boil. Cook for 3 minutes, then drain into a colander and shake dry.

Preheat the oven to 220°C fan/240°C/gas mark 9. Arrange the cabbage and sprouts with the red onion in a large roasting dish (e.g. 25 x 37cm), drizzle over the olive oil, lightly season and roast for 25 minutes, stirring halfway through. Mix in the diced cheese, return the dish to the oven for another few minutes, and serve straight away.

A lovely succulent gratin, in fact the only dry land in sight is the crispy breadcrumb layer on top, and even then there's still plenty of call for a baguette to mop up all the sweet oily juices.

gratin of tomatoes and goat's cheese

extra virgin olive oil

1 red onion, peeled, halved
   and thinly sliced

1.1kg tomatoes

4 Crottins de Chavignol (60g each),
   or other semi-matured goat's cheese

sea salt, black pepper

1 tablespoon fresh thyme leaves

2 garlic cloves, peeled
   and finely chopped

40g fresh white or sourdough
   breadcrumbs

Serves 6

Preheat a tablespoon of oil in a large frying pan over a medium heat. Add the onion and cook for 6–7 minutes until golden, stirring occasionally, then transfer it to a bowl. Bring a large pan of water to the boil. Cut out a cone from the top of each tomato, dunk them into the boiling water for about 20 seconds, and then into cold water. Slip off the skins and thinly slice them across. Likewise thinly slice the Crottins into rounds, discarding the end rinds – you should get four or five slices from each one.

Assemble the gratin in a 30cm gratin dish or other shallow ovenproof dish of a similar size. Arrange half the tomatoes and goat's cheese in overlapping slices in rows, so you have a couple of slices of tomato to each one of goat's cheese (reserve the ends of tomato until last, as you probably won't need them, and they can be saved for some other use). Season and scatter over half the thyme and garlic, then trickle over a tablespoon of oil. Repeat this layer.

Scatter the onion over the top, then toss the breadcrumbs with a tablespoon of oil, and scatter over. You can prepare the gratin to this point up to about an hour in advance.

Heat the oven to 190°C fan/210°C/gas mark 6, and bake the gratin for 35–40 minutes, until golden and crisp. Leave it to stand for 10 minutes before serving.

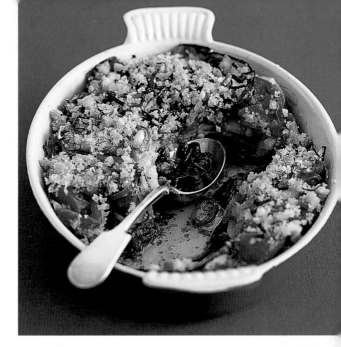

Despite its Provençal credentials, the combination of aubergines and tomatoes cannot but fail to transport us to a Mamma Mia-perfect craggy Greek coastline. Either way we're beside the Mediterranean, toasting the setting sun with a rough white wine, and that leads to thoughts of crispy red mullet or sardines hot from the grill, or some barbecued lamb.

provençal gratin

2 medium aubergines
extra virgin olive oil
sea salt, black pepper
600g maincrop potatoes, peeled
3 garlic cloves, peeled and
   crushed to a paste
2 beefsteak tomatoes
   (600–700g)
1 red onion, peeled, halved
   and thinly sliced
75g fresh white breadcrumbs
3 tablespoons fresh marjoram
   or oregano leaves

Serves 4–6

Preheat the oven to 180°C fan /200°C/gas mark 6. Cut the aubergines across into slices 1cm thick, discarding the ends. Heat a large frying pan, or even better two. Brush one side of each slice of aubergine with oil, season and fry this side until golden. Brush the top side with oil, turn and fry this side too. As the slices are cooked, arrange them in overlapping rows in a 30 x 20cm gratin dish (ideally cast iron).

Slice the potatoes as thinly as possible – a food processor fitted with a fine slicing attachment makes light work of this. Toss them in a bowl with 2 tablespoons of olive oil, the garlic and some seasoning. Lay them, overlapping, on top of the aubergines. Don't worry too much about looks here as they'll be concealed by the next layer – as long as they lie evenly that's fine. Press down with your hands. Cover tightly with foil and bake for about 45 minutes, until the potatoes are tender when pierced with a knife.

In the meantime, bring a pan of water to the boil. Cut out a cone from the top of each tomato to remove the core and plunge them into the water for about 20 seconds, then into cold water. Slip off their skins and slice them across, discarding the bottom slices or keeping them for some other use. Lay the sliced tomatoes in overlapping rows on top of the potato and season. Scatter over the onion and drizzle over 2 tablespoons of oil. Toss the breadcrumbs with another couple of tablespoons of oil and scatter these over, then the marjoram or oregano. Give everything a final drizzle of oil. Turn the oven up to 200°C fan/220°C/gas mark 7 and pop the gratin back in for another 20–25 minutes, until golden. The gratin can be successfully reheated for 20–25 minutes in a medium oven.

Just the one layer of butternut squash here that cooks to a gorgeously melting consistency between two layer of tatties. For life beyond Swiss Gruyère, look to their French equivalents Beaufort, Comte and Abondance, also Swiss Appenzeller, all are strong cheeses that succeed in being delicate and elegant at the same time.

gratin of butternut squash, potato and gruyère

2 x 600g butternut squashes
800g maincrop potatoes
4 tablespoons extra virgin olive oil
3 garlic cloves, peeled and crushed
    to a paste
sea salt, black pepper
a handful of fresh sage leaves
4 tablespoons double cream
150g grated Gruyère

Serves 6

Preheat the oven to 180°C fan/200°C/gas mark 6. Cut the skin off the squashes, then cut off the trunks and thinly slice into rounds. Halve the bulb, cut out the seeds and thinly slice into crescents.

Peel and slice the potatoes as thinly as possible, discarding the ends – you can use the slicing attachment on a food processor for this. Toss them in a large bowl with half each of the olive oil and garlic, and some seasoning. Toss the squash with the remaining olive oil, garlic and some seasoning in another large bowl. Lay half the potatoes in rows of overlapping slices in a 20 x 30cm gratin dish or shallow ovenproof dish of a similar size. Lay the squash on top, first arranging the round pieces in rows of overlapping slices, then fitting the crescents on top as neatly as possible. Top with a final layer of potatoes. Press down with your hands, but don't worry if it seems a little bulky, it will sink as it cooks. Cover tightly with foil and bake for 50 minutes, until the gratin is tender when pierced with a knife.

Turn the oven up to 200°C fan/220°C/gas mark 7. Lay the sage leaves on top of the gratin, drizzle over the cream and scatter over the cheese. Return the gratin to the oven for 15–25 minutes, until the cheese is golden and bubbling. It can also be cooked in advance and reheated in an oven preheated to 200°C fan/220°C/gas mark 7 for 20 minutes.

As good eaten cold as hot, when all the punchy Mediterranean flavours shine through. Try to buy a really good pesto from a deli if not making your own, then you can pick up the necessary loaf of bread while you're there.

roasted pepper, goat's cheese and pesto gratin

8 red peppers

4 tomatoes

3 tablespoons extra virgin olive oil

sea salt, black pepper

200g goat's cheese, rind removed, thinly sliced

4 tablespoons pesto

Serves 4–6

Preheat the oven to 180°C fan/200°C/gas mark 6, and roast the peppers on an oven rack for 20 minutes. Place them inside a plastic bag (you may like to put this inside another plastic bag to make sure it doesn't leak), wrap the bag up and set aside for several hours or overnight to cool.

Skin the peppers, discarding the core and seeds. If necessary give them a quick rinse under the cold tap, then cut them into wide strips. Bring a small pan of water to the boil and cut out a cone from the top of each tomato to remove the core. Plunge them into the boiling water for about 20 seconds and then into cold water. Slip off the skins and slice them.

Heat the oven to 200°C fan/220°C/gas mark 7. Drizzle 1 tablespoon of oil over the base of a 30cm oval gratin dish or other shallow ovenproof dish of a similar size. Arrange half the peppers over the base and season them. Lay half the goat's cheese over, then the sliced tomatoes, and spoon over half the pesto. Lay the remaining peppers in place, season them and scatter over the remaining goat's cheese. Dollop over the rest of the pesto and another couple of tablespoons of olive oil and bake for 25–30 minutes. Serve warm rather than piping hot, about 30 minutes out of the oven, or at room temperature.

Anything that's finely sliced and cooked to within a whisker of collapse enters the comfort zone. But this is pretty healthy to boot, deceptively creamy, though in essence a mass of tender wintery roots with a little melted cheese and some crisp breadcrumbs.

root vegetable and cheddar gratin

450–500g carrots, trimmed, peeled
   and thinly sliced
450–500g parsnips, trimmed, peeled
   and thinly sliced
450–500g leeks (trimmed weight), thinly sliced
250ml vegetable stock
30g unsalted butter, diced
sea salt, black pepper
1½ teaspoons caster sugar
4 medium eggs
100g grated mature Cheddar
50g fresh white breadcrumbs
2 tablespoons groundnut
   or vegetable oil
6 tablespoons coarsely chopped
   fresh flat-leaf parsley

Serves 6

Place the carrots, parsnips and leeks in a large saucepan with the stock, butter, 1½ teaspoons of salt and the sugar and bring the liquid to the boil. Cover the pan and cook over a medium heat for 5 minutes, then cook uncovered for another 15 minutes, stirring occasionally, until nearly all the liquid has evaporated and the vegetables are sitting in a buttery emulsion. Leave to cool for a few minutes.

Whisk the eggs in a large bowl with some seasoning, then stir in two-thirds of the cheese. Toss the breadcrumbs in another bowl with the oil, then mix in the rest of the cheese. Add the vegetables to the bowl with the egg and cheese mixture, scatter over the parsley and stir to combine everything. Tip the mixture into a 30cm oval gratin dish or other shallow ovenproof dish of a similar size. Smooth the surface and scatter the breadcrumb mixture on top. The gratin can be made up to this point several hours in advance, in which case scatter the breadcrumbs over at the last minute, cover and chill.

Preheat the oven to 200°C fan/220°C/gas mark 7. Place the gratin dish in a roasting dish with boiling water coming two-thirds of the way up the sides, and bake for 30–35 minutes, until the breadcrumbs are golden and crusty. Serve straight away.

This is a celebration of all the young vegetables that appear in the spring – lightly cooked and coated in a creamy béchamel sauce and lots of cheese.

gratin of spring veg

750g young or baby turnips, romanesco florets, carrots and courgettes, trimmed and peeled if necessary
150ml white wine
50g unsalted butter
40g plain flour
300ml milk
175ml double cream
1 bay leaf
sea salt, black pepper
180g Gruyère, sliced

Serves 6

Preheat the oven to 190°C fan/210°C/gas mark 6. Bring a large pan of salted water to the boil. Depending on the size of the turnips, quarter or cut them into wedges, and do the same with the baby romanescos. Add the turnips and carrots to the pan and cook for about 7 minutes, adding the courgettes and romanesco quarters 3 minutes before the end. Drain them into a colander and leave for a few minutes for the surface water to evaporate.

In the meantime, make the sauce. Pour the wine into a small non-stick saucepan and reduce to a third of its volume, then transfer it to a bowl. Melt the butter in the same pan, add the flour and cook the roux for 1–2 minutes. Gradually incorporate the milk, cream and reduced wine off the heat, whisking to disperse any lumps, then add the bay leaf. Return to the heat and simmer for 5 minutes, stirring occasionally, then season with salt and pepper.

Arrange the vegetables with the sauce and the cheese in a 30cm oval gratin dish or other shallow ovenproof dish of an equivalent size, discarding the bay leaf. Bake for 30–35 minutes, until golden and bubbling at the edges. Spoon off any buttery fat on the surface before serving.

Crusty top and bottom and a fluffy mash in between, set with teasing little pockets of salty Cheddar. I always get huge pleasure out of marrying this mash with roast chicken, or a lamb shoulder studded with garlic and rosemary. When so often the great Swiss cheeses get the upper hand, it's satisfying to sit down to something more British.

cheese soufflé mash

Mash

1kg maincrop potatoes,
    peeled and cut into even chunks
50g salted butter, diced,
    plus extra for greasing
6 tablespoons freshly grated Parmesan
200ml full-cream milk
sea salt, black pepper
freshly grated nutmeg
3 medium egg whites
200g mature Cheddar, cut into
    1cm dice

Herb Salad

50g rocket leaves (ideally wild)
3 tablespoons each of small fresh
    flat-leaf parsley and mint leaves
3 spring onions, trimmed and cut into
    fine strips about 5cm long
4–6 tablespoons extra virgin olive oil
1 teaspoon lemon juice
sea salt

Serves 4–6

Bring a large pan of salted water to the boil, add the potatoes and simmer until tender.

Preheat the oven to 200°C fan/220°C/gas mark 7. Generously butter a 30cm oval gratin dish or other ovenproof dish of a similar size and dust it with a couple of tablespoons of grated Parmesan.

Drain the potatoes into a colander, then pass through a mouli-légumes or sieve into a large bowl. Add the butter, and once this has melted stir in the milk, some seasoning and a grating of nutmeg. You should have a sloppy mash. Whisk the egg whites in a medium bowl until stiff, using an electric whisk, and fold these into the mash in two goes, followed by the diced cheese. Taste to check the seasoning. Transfer the mixture into the prepared dish, scatter over the rest of the Parmesan and bake for 20–25 minutes, until puffy and golden. Serve straight away with the herb salad below – you want to capture all those little cheese pockets while they're gooey.

To make the herb salad, toss the rocket and herbs in a bowl and mix in the spring onions. Serve a pile of this on top of each serving of potato, and drizzle over a tablespoon of olive oil, squeeze over a little lemon and scatter over a few flakes of sea salt.

Pasta gratins begin and end with macaroni cheese, with everything in between
being a homage. Here rigatoni – the four by four of macaroni – takes centre stage,
and lip-service is paid to a few veggies by way of fried aubergine and a tomato sauce.
But it's still macaroni cheese.

gratin of rigatoni with aubergine and mozzarella

Béchamel

50g unsalted butter

40g flour

500ml full-cream milk

sea salt, black pepper

1 bay leaf

75g freshly grated Parmesan

Gratin

extra virgin olive oil

2 aubergines, sliced 1cm thick

250g rigatoni

2 buffalo mozzarellas, drained
   and sliced

30g breadcrumbs

Tomato Sauce

1 dried red chilli, finely chopped

4 garlic cloves, peeled and chopped

6 tablespoons chopped fresh
   flat-leaf parsley

400ml passata

Serves 4

To make the béchamel, melt the butter in a small non-stick saucepan over a medium heat, stir in the flour and allow the roux to seethe for about a minute. Working off the heat, gradually incorporate the milk using a wooden spoon, a little at a time to begin with. Season the sauce, add the bay leaf, bring to the boil stirring frequently and simmer for 10 minutes, giving it a stir every now and again. If it seems at all lumpy at the end, give it a quick whisk. Discard the bay leaf and stir in the Parmesan.

Heat a large frying pan over a medium heat. You will need to cook the aubergine slices in batches. Brush one side with olive oil, season, and fry oiled side down until golden. Brush the top side with oil, turn and fry until golden too. Remove and repeat with the remaining aubergines.

At the same time, bring a large pan of salted water to the boil. Add the pasta and give it a stir. Cook until almost tender, on the firm side of al dente, then drain into a colander and briefly run cold water through it. Return it to the pan and toss with a tablespoon of olive oil.

To make the tomato sauce, heat 1 tablespoon of oil in a clean frying pan over a medium heat, add the chilli and garlic, and as soon as it starts to colour add the parsley and stir to coat it in oil. Pour in the passata and season. Bring to the boil and simmer for a couple of minutes.

Preheat the oven to 180°C fan/200°C/gas mark 6. To assemble the gratin, coat the base of a 20 x 30cm roasting dish with a couple of tablespoons of the tomato sauce. Layer half the pasta on top, then half each of the tomato sauce, aubergines and mozzarella. Repeat with the remaining half of the ingredients.

Give the béchamel a quick whisk and smooth it over the surface. Toss the breadcrumbs with a tablespoon of oil and some seasoning and scatter over the top.* Bake the gratin for 35 minutes, until the surface is golden and bubbling.

* This gratin can be prepared to this point in advance, in which case cover it with clingfilm, leave it to cool completely and then chill. It may need a little longer in the oven.

green mains

This chapter could be seen as an impostor, given that so many of the dishes in this book will stand in as mains. Most of us will be quite happy with a gratin or a gorgeous big salad for supper with no further ado. But every now and again, especially if you've got someone coming round to lunch or supper and want a green 'main' dish that is very obviously a main dish and has that finger-clicking demand for attendant salads, then a lovely tart, a pie or a big omelette has a certain presence.

I've always derived enormous satisfaction from making tarts – while bread-making is altogether forbidding to the techno-shy, these boost your confidence in inverse proportion to your skill. Anyone can make pastry. But before we get to that point, we have the joys of ready-made puff, which makes for the simplest of pizza-style miniature tarts for eating in-hand. And it extends its talents to large oblong tarts, such as the one laid out with neat rows of asparagus spears. But the real spectacular is the mushroom Pithivier with its scalloped edges, which belongs somewhere in a salon with all things Louis XIV.

Returning to hands-on skill, you will actually get better results making pastry in a food processor than by hand. This leads on to classic quiche-type tarts such as spinach and Gruyère, so hackneyed it is all too easy to forget just how good it can be. With such tarts it's a case of how you serve them and not when you serve them; they're fab at any time, brunch onwards.

The same compliments can be paid to frittate, a winning Italian way with eggs that bypasses the usual sleight of hand called for in flipping or rolling them out of the pan. They are cooked first on the hob in a frying pan and then under the grill until they are puffy and golden. Like tortes, which are something like a quiche without the pastry layered into a cake tin, they spill their largesse from messy puffed edges. Both emerge impressively golden and crusty.

These little pizzettas tend to be preyed upon by wandering fingers long before they are cool, but they can be eaten cold, and are great for picnics or cut into nibble-size quarters with a pre-prandial drink.

cherry tomato pizzettas

300g puff pastry
Dijon mustard
300g cherry tomatoes, halved
1 egg yolk, blended with
  1 tablespoon water
sea salt, black pepper
30g finely shaved Parmesan
extra virgin olive oil

Serves 6

Preheat the oven to 200°C fan/220°C/gas mark 7. Thinly roll out the pastry on a lightly floured work surface, half at a time if it's easier, and cut out 6 x 12cm circles using a bowl or plate as a guide. Arrange these on a couple of baking trays.

Spread a little Dijon mustard in the centre of each circle, to within about 2cm of the rim. Place the tomatoes on top. Brush the surrounding rim with the eggwash, then season the tomatoes, cover with a few shavings of Parmesan, drizzle over a little olive oil and bake for 15–20 minutes, until golden and risen. Serve hot or cold.

Cut into wedges these make lovely appetisers, as well as serving as a light lunch or a prelude to a heavier one. They are at their prettiest made with red chicory.

chicory, prune and blue cheese pizzettas

500g puff pastry

120g Fourme d'Ambert, diced

100g stoned prunes (no-need-to-
  soak variety), sliced

2–3 heads of red or white chicory
  (depending on size), base trimmed
  and outer leaves discarded

2 tablespoons extra virgin olive oil

sea salt, black pepper

1 egg yolk, blended with
  1 tablespoon water

coarsely chopped fresh flat-leaf parsley
  to serve

Serves 6

Thinly roll out the pastry on a lightly floured work surface, half at a time if it's easier, and cut out 6 x 12cm circles using a bowl or plate as a guide. Combine the cheese and prunes in a large bowl.

To finish making the tarts, preheat the oven to 200°C fan/220°C/gas mark 7. Arrange the pastry bases on two large baking sheets. Halve the chicory heads, cut them into long thin strips and halve again if longer than about 7cm. Toss these with the cheese and prunes, the olive oil and some seasoning. Pile the mixture into the centre of the tarts, leaving a 1–2cm rim. Brush this with the eggwash and bake for 15–20 minutes, until the pastry rim is golden and risen and the filling has begun to colour. Scatter over some parsley, and serve straight away, or warm about 20 minutes later. They can also be reheated. In this case save scattering over the parsley until the last minute.

Leeks, like onions, roast up a treat. A spell in the oven concentrates their sweetness, making salty feta a perfect partner.

leek and feta pizzettas

25g unsalted butter
2 tablespoons extra virgin olive oil
3 leeks, trimmed and thinly sliced
sea salt, black pepper
1 tablespoon fresh lemon thyme leaves
300g puff pastry
120g feta, crumbled or diced
coarsely chopped fresh flat-leaf
   parsley to serve

Serves 6

Preheat the oven to 200°C fan/220°C/gas mark 7. Melt the butter in a large frying pan over a medium heat with half the olive oil, and once the froth subsides add the leeks. Season and fry for a few minutes until softened, without colouring, then stir in the thyme.

Thinly roll out the pastry on a lightly floured work surface, half at a time if it's easier, and cut out 6 x 12cm circles using a bowl or plate as a guide. Arrange these on a couple of baking trays.

Gently fold the cheese into the leeks. Scatter this over the pastry circles to within 1cm of the rim, drizzle over 1 tablespoon of oil and bake for 15 minutes. Serve hot or at room temperature, scattered with parsley. They can also be reheated.

Homage to those big pans of filo tart with spinach and feta that grace the rickety tables of seaside Greek tavernas beneath scanty bamboo mats for shade.

summer leaf filo pie

650g young spinach leaves
2 tablespoons extra virgin olive oil
4 leeks, trimmed and sliced
1 tablespoon fresh thyme leaves
sea salt, black pepper
100g unsalted butter, melted,
   plus 25g
4 garlic cloves, peeled
   and finely chopped
25g fresh flat-leaf parsley,
   coarsely chopped
25g watercress, coarsely chopped
300g feta, cut into 1cm dice
1 x 250g packet of filo pastry

Serves 6

Bring a large pan of salted water to the boil. Add half the spinach and blanch it for 2 minutes, then transfer it to a colander in the sink using a slotted spatula and repeat with the remainder. Using a potato masher, press out as much of the water as possible – it's important to remove all the excess so that the pastry doesn't go soggy when it's cooked.

At the same time, heat the olive oil in a large frying pan over a medium heat. Add the leeks, thyme and some seasoning and fry them for 5–10 minutes until soft and lightly coloured, stirring now and again. Transfer them to a large bowl.

Melt the 25g of butter in the pan you cooked the leeks in over a medium heat. Add the garlic and briefly fry until aromatic, then add the spinach, season, and cook for a few minutes to infuse it with the garlic, stirring occasionally. Add to the bowl with the leeks and leave to cool.

To cook the pie, preheat the oven to 180°C fan/200°C/gas mark 6. To finish preparing the filling, mix the chopped parsley, watercress and feta into the cooked vegetables. Lay the pile of filo pastry out on the work surface and select a 20 x 30cm baking dish. Using this as a guide, trim the pile of pastry, using a sharp knife, so it is 1cm larger than the top of the dish, allowing for shrinkage.

Paint the bottom of the dish with melted butter, then paint the top sheet of pastry, lay it in place, and repeat until you have about seven sheets layered – they will come a little of the way up the sides of the dish. Spoon the filling evenly over the pastry, and layer with another seven sheets of pastry, again painting each one with butter before laying it in place. Using a sharp knife, score the top sheet into six squares and bake the pie for 40 minutes. Serve straight away, while the pastry is crisp.

Made as a big slab on a baking tray, this plays on the graphic beauty of asparagus to form neat lines and rectangles, so contrary to most food. That said it's messier to eat than it looks, and it's paper napkins all round.

asparagus tray tart

450g finger-thick asparagus spears
250g puff pastry
2 medium egg yolks
150ml crème fraîche
½ teaspoon Dijon mustard
2 tablespoons freshly grated Parmesan
sea salt, black pepper

Serves 4

Preheat the oven to 190°C fan/210°C/gas mark 6. Bring a large pan of salted water to the boil. Trim the asparagus spears where they begin to become woody and peel to within 2cm of the tip. Add to the pan, bring back to the boil and cook for 4 minutes. Drain and refresh in cold water. Remove and dry on a tea towel.

Roll the pastry a few millimetres thick into a rectangle 40 x 20cm and trim to neaten the edges – make sure you have a baking sheet large enough, otherwise adjust the dimensions accordingly. Lay the pastry on the baking sheet, and lay the asparagus in rows of single spears, so there is a pastry surround of 2cm. Beat the egg yolks and paint the pastry border. Bake the tart for 15 minutes.

Blend the crème fraîche, mustard, Parmesan, remaining beaten egg yolks and seasoning together in a bowl. Spoon this cream over the asparagus and bake for another 15 minutes until golden on the top. Serve 5 minutes out of the oven, though it is also excellent cold.

Bubble and squeak is one of very few home-grown peasant dishes that remain a part of our repertoire. And yet for a rustic dish it's surprisingly difficult to get right, or at least as good as I recall from my childhood. This pie has all the comfort: cabbage with potato is a wonderfully soothing marriage of humble leaf and spud. Your cabbage should be dark in hue with a lively bitterness – anything blond will be too tame.

bubble and squeak pie

600g medium waxy potatoes, peeled
120g leafy greens (trimmed weight)
25g salted butter
1 onion, peeled and chopped
sea salt, white pepper
500g puff pastry
200g Lancashire, crumbled
1 egg yolk blended with
   1 tablespoon water

Serves 6

Bring two large pans of salted water to the boil. Add the potatoes to one and simmer until tender, then drain them into a colander and leave for a few minutes to steam dry. Add the greens to the other pan, simmer for 3 minutes, then drain and leave to cool.

Melt the butter in a large frying pan over a medium heat. Add the onion and fry for several minutes until softened, stirring occasionally and without colouring. Coarsely mash the potatoes using a fork or a potato masher, then mix in the onion and the butter it cooked in, season with a little salt and white pepper and leave to cool.

Preheat the oven to 180°C fan/200°C/gas mark 6. Roll out two-thirds of the pastry on a lightly floured work surface to fit the inside of a 23cm tart tin, 5–6cm deep with a removable base, so it is large enough to drape over the sides. Lay it in place and trim the top. Fold the cheese into the potato and onion mixture. Scatter half of this over the base of the tart, gently press the mixture down, lay the cabbage leaves in a layer on top, lightly season, then scatter over the rest of the potato.

Roll out the remaining pastry to fit the top (you can use the tin as a guide) and lay it over the potato. Brush the surface with the eggwash, then fold the rim down to seal the pie and brush this edge with eggwash too. Cut four slits in the surface in the shape of a cross, to within a couple of centimetres of the centre. You can make the pie several hours in advance, in which case chill it. Bake for 40 minutes and serve hot or warm.

Pithiviers are splendid pies to behold, with their glazed domes and scalloped edges. The original of a sweet creamy frangipane sets the tone for other fillings, such as this rich wild mushroom purée. I would serve this with a salad of baby spinach dressed with extra virgin olive oil and balsamic vinegar, and with coarsely chopped toasted hazelnuts.

mushroom and herb pithivier

1kg mixed mushrooms (e.g.
   chestnut, Portabello, shiitake),
   trimmed
60g unsalted butter
4 shallots, peeled
   and finely chopped
sea salt, black pepper
125g cream cheese
2 teaspoons finely chopped
   fresh tarragon
2 tablespoons snipped fresh chives
375g puff pastry
1 egg yolk, blended with
   1 tablespoon milk

Serves 6

Finely chop the mushrooms in a food processor, working in batches to avoid reducing them to a complete mush. Melt the butter in two large frying pans over a medium heat, and cook the mushrooms with the shallots and some seasoning for 12–15 minutes, stirring frequently, until the mixture is dry and pieces of mushroom begin to separate out. Transfer the mushroom purée to a bowl, cover and leave it to cool, then blend in the cream cheese and herbs and taste for seasoning.

Thinly roll out half the pastry on a lightly floured work surface. Lay it on a baking sheet and, using a 20cm cake tin or plate, mark a circle in the centre. Smooth the mushroom purée inside the circle, using a palette knife to shape it into a disc. Roll out the remaining half of the pastry, brush the rim of the pie with the eggwash and lay the sheet on top, smoothing it over the mushroom filling and pressing the edges together. Now cut around the rim in a scalloped shape – it should look a little like a flower. You can prepare the pie to this point several hours in advance, in which case cover and chill it.

Preheat the oven to 180°C fan/200°C/gas mark 6. Brush the top of the pie all over with the eggwash and then, using the tip of a sharp knife, trace lines on the top and the scallops at the side (traditionally these are curved). Bake the pie for 30 minutes and serve hot or warm. The pie can also be reheated.

An early summer tart with so many peas it leaves you in no doubt that good weather is on the way. Packs of fresh shelled peas are the greatest convenience since frozen, my one gripe being that we hardly ever see them in the pod any longer. It's such a pleasure popping open those smooth green pods and running your finger along the insides to extract the peas within, which are at their sweetest in the short time before you cook them.

pea, feta and basil tart

25g unsalted butter
½ teaspoon caster sugar
sea salt, black pepper
600g fresh shelled peas
2 medium eggs, plus 1 yolk
300ml whipping cream
150g freshly grated Parmesan
150g feta, cut into 1cm dice
a handful of fresh basil leaves,
    torn into 2 or 3
1 x 23cm tart case, 5–6cm deep,
    pre-baked (see page 81)
1 tablespoon extra virgin olive oil

Serves 6

Preheat the oven to 180°C fan/200°C/gas mark 6. Place 150ml water in a large saucepan with the butter, sugar and ½ teaspoon of salt. Bring to the boil over a high heat, add the peas and cook for 5 minutes, stirring occasionally, until tender. Drain them into a sieve. Place half of them in a food processor and briefly whiz to break them up.

Whisk the eggs and yolk with the cream, some seasoning and half the Parmesan in a large bowl. Fold in all the peas, half the feta and the basil. Transfer the filling to the tart case and scatter over the remaining feta and Parmesan. Drizzle the olive oil over the surface and bake the tart for 35–40 minutes, until golden and set in the centre. Leave to cool for 20 minutes before serving. This tart is also good eaten at room temperature, and can be reheated.

The texture of this tart is positively exquisite, but its success lies in squeezing out every last drop of liquid from the cooked spinach to ensure it sets properly.

spinach and gruyère tart

800g spinach, washed
300ml whipping cream
3 medium eggs
sea salt, black pepper
freshly grated nutmeg
200g grated Gruyère
1 x 23cm tart case, 5–6cm deep,
    pre-baked (see opposite page)
120g cherry tomatoes, halved
groundnut oil

Serves 6

Preheat the oven to 180°C fan/200°C/gas mark 6. You may need to cook the spinach in two pans, or in two batches. Place it in a large saucepan with just the water that clings to the leaves from washing, cover with a lid and steam over a medium heat for 10 minutes, stirring it halfway through, until it collapses. Drain it into a sieve, and press out as much liquid as possible using a potato masher. Either leave it to cool, or, using rubber gloves, squeeze balls of the spinach between your hands to extract every last trace of moisture, then slice it.

Whisk the cream, eggs, some seasoning and a little grated nutmeg in a bowl. Stir in the spinach, making sure it is evenly distributed, and then half the Gruyère. Transfer this to the tart case and smooth the surface. Toss the cherry tomatoes in a bowl with just enough oil to coat them and a little seasoning. Scatter these over the surface of the tart and press them into the filling to level them with the spinach. Scatter over the remaining cheese, mainly towards the centre, and bake for 35–45 minutes, until golden on the surface and set. Leave to cool for 10–20 minutes before serving. While it is best eaten hot or warm from the oven, it does reheat successfully.

shortcrust pastry for a 23cm tart case

225g plain flour
a pinch of sea salt
150g unsalted butter, chilled
and diced
1 medium egg, separated

Place the flour and salt in the bowl of a food processor, add the butter and reduce to a fine crumb-like consistency. Incorporate the egg yolk, and then with the motor running trickle in just enough cold water for the dough to cling together into lumps. Transfer the pastry to a large bowl and bring it together into a ball, using your hands.

Wrap the pastry in clingfilm and chill for at least 1 hour. It will keep well in the fridge for up to a couple of days.

Preheat the oven to 180°C fan/200°C/gas mark 6. Knead the pastry until it is pliable. Thinly roll it out on a lightly floured surface and carefully lift it into a 23cm tart tin with a removable base. This is quite a durable pastry and shouldn't tear or collapse. Press it into the corners of the tin and run a rolling pin over the top to trim the edges. Reserve the trimmings for patching the pastry case after it is baked. Prick the base with a fork and line it with a sheet of foil, tucking it over the top to secure the pastry sides to the tin. Now weight it with baking beans – dried pulses will do nicely.

Bake the pastry case for 15 minutes, then remove the foil and baking beans. If any of the sides have shrunk more than they should, use a little of the reserved pastry to patch them, bearing in mind that the tart can only be filled as far as the lowest point of the sides. Brush the base and sides of the case with the reserved egg white, then bake it for another 10 minutes until it is lightly coloured. This glaze helps to seal the pastry and prevent the filling soaking in.

tart tins

Given that pastry sometimes shrinks, it is a good idea to start off with a tart tin 5–6cm deep. Failing that, you could forgo the crimped edges and use a cake tin with a removable collar – you can always trim the sides after cooking if they seem too deep. But I'd avoid china quiche dishes, which are rarely deep enough and make it difficult to serve the tart without damaging it.

These little omelettes with their lacy golden edges are delicious tucked inside a warm pocket of pitta bread, or eaten with a green or tomato salad, as well as being ripe for nibbling in hand.

pea and parmesan fritters

Fritters

extra virgin olive oil

sea salt, black pepper

½ teaspoon caster sugar

200g fresh shelled peas

4 medium eggs

1 tablespoon lemon juice

75g freshly grated Parmesan

4 tablespoons coarsely chopped
   fresh flat-leaf parsley, plus extra
   to serve

Salad

rocket leaves

extra virgin olive oil

a squeeze of lemon juice

sea salt

a handful of Parmesan shavings

Serves 4

Place 2 tablespoons of olive oil in a medium saucepan with 3 tablespoons of water, ½ teaspoon of salt and the sugar. Bring this to a simmer over a high heat, then add the peas. Cook, tossing occasionally, for about 3 minutes until just tender, then drain.

Whisk the eggs in a large bowl with the lemon juice and some seasoning, and fold in the grated Parmesan, the peas and parsley. You can do this a short time in advance.

Heat a large non-stick frying pan over a high heat, add about 1 teaspoon of oil, and drop tablespoons of the mixture into the pan, spreading them out into omelettes 10cm in diameter. Cook for about 1 minute each side, until really golden. You will need to do this in batches, draining them on a double thickness of kitchen paper as you go, and adding more oil to the pan as necessary.

Either transfer them to a serving plate and scatter over a little more parsley, or serve piled with the salad below.

a little salad

Toss the rocket leaves with enough olive oil to coat them in a bowl, and season with a squeeze of lemon juice and a pinch of salt. Divide the fritters between four plates, pile the salad on top, scatter over a few Parmesan shavings and drizzle over a little more oil.

Basil, Parmesan and courgettes could charm the most jaded palate, and baby courgettes have the edge here over anything larger.

courgette frittata

350g baby courgettes, ends trimmed,
   halved lengthways
3 tablespoons extra virgin olive oil
sea salt, black pepper
6 medium eggs
50g freshly grated Parmesan
a large handful of fresh basil leaves,
   torn in half
25g finely sliced Parmesan

Serves 4

Heat a ridged griddle over a medium heat for several minutes. Place the halved courgettes in a large bowl, drizzle over 2 tablespoons of olive oil, add some seasoning and toss to coat them. If necessary, cook the courgettes in batches, turning them as they colour on the underside and cooking the second side. Remove them to a plate – they don't have to be completely cool before the next stage, but equally they can be cooked in advance if wished.

Whisk the eggs in a bowl and stir in the grated Parmesan, basil leaves and some seasoning. Fold in the grilled courgettes. Heat the grill to high, and also heat a 26cm frying pan with a heatproof handle over a medium heat. Add a tablespoon of oil to the pan, tip in the egg and courgette mixture and cook for 3 minutes. Scatter the Parmesan slices over the top of the omelette, drizzle over another tablespoon of oil and place under the grill for 3–4 minutes, until golden and puffy at the sides. The frittata can be eaten hot or at room temperature.

This is for all those who feel Spanish omelettes are never quite deep enough. A springform cake tin ensures the Vi-Spring-like luxury of layers you didn't even dream existed until you took your fork to it.

a very deep spanish omelette

Heat 2 tablespoons of olive oil in a large frying pan over a medium heat. Add the potatoes and cook for about 5 minutes, turning them now and again to coat them in the oil. Season with salt, add 150ml of water to the pan, cover with a large lid and cook over a low heat for about 10 minutes, until the potatoes are just tender. Using the lid, drain off any excess water and leave to cool, covered.

Heat another couple of tablespoons of oil in a large saucepan over a medium heat. Add the onions and sweat them for 15–20 minutes, stirring frequently, until golden and silky. Season them, transfer to a bowl and leave to cool.

Preheat the oven to 180°C fan/200°C/gas mark 6. Use the butter to grease a 20cm cake tin, 6cm deep, with a removable base and dust it with a little grated Parmesan. Whisk the eggs and egg yolks, cream, parsley, half the remaining Parmesan and some seasoning together in a bowl. Coat the base of the tin with a few tablespoons of this mixture, then use half the remainder to coat the potato slices, and mix the rest in with the onions. Lay half the potato slices over the base of the tin, spooning over half the egg, then the onions, then the rest of the potato slices and egg mixture. Scatter over the remaining Parmesan and bake for 45–50 minutes, until golden on the surface and set (you can check this by inserting a knife into the centre – if it seems runny, give it a little longer, and if necessary you can cover the top with foil to stop it from colouring further). Run a knife around the collar of the omelette and leave it to cool to room temperature, when it will firm up. Serve it in wedges.

4 tablespoons extra virgin olive oil
1kg medium waxy potatoes, peeled and thickly sliced
sea salt, black pepper
5 onions, peeled, halved and sliced
a knob of unsalted butter
150g freshly grated Parmesan
3 medium eggs, plus 2 yolks
300ml double cream
3 tablespoons coarsely chopped fresh flat-leaf parsley

Serves 6

Wild mushrooms are principally to do with perfume – if it is texture you are after, then flat-caps will serve you just as well. So when you need a largish quantity the best route is to take advantage of both. It doesn't have to be any particular type of fungi, whatever's on offer and the purse allows.

wild mushroom torte

50g unsalted butter

150g freshly grated Parmesan

4 tablespoons extra virgin olive oil

2 shallots, peeled and finely chopped

800g mixture of wild and cultivated
  mushrooms, trimmed and finely
  sliced

sea salt, black pepper

225ml double cream

3 tablespoons chopped fresh
  flat-leaf parsley

2 medium eggs, plus 1 egg yolk,
  whisked

Serves 6

Preheat the oven to 190°C fan/210°C/gas mark 6. Liberally butter a 20cm cake tin, 6cm deep, with a removable base and dust it with grated Parmesan. You will need to cook the mushrooms in about four batches. Heat a quarter of the remaining butter with a tablespoon of olive oil in a large frying pan, add some of the chopped shallots, and once they have softened add a quarter of the mushrooms. Fry them, stirring frequently, until they soften and start to colour, seasoning them towards the end. Remove them to a bowl and cook the remainder in the same fashion.

Transfer half of the cooked mushrooms to a food processor and reduce to a textured purée. Combine this with the rest of the mushrooms in a large bowl. Stir in the cream, parsley, eggs, half the remaining Parmesan and some seasoning.

Transfer this mixture to the prepared tin, scatter over the remaining Parmesan and bake for 35–40 minutes, until golden on the surface and set. I like the torte best about 10 minutes out of the oven, though it can also be eaten at room temperature. Run a knife around the collar to remove it, and serve in wedges.

Large pumpkins baked in this fashion make for a full-on earthy, rustic extravaganza. But the bigger they get the more at risk you are of them bursting at the sides as they cook, which is a very messy business. This bijou take plays it safe with baby pumpkins, and you get your very own to dip into, which is always a plus. Basically any small round thick-skinned pumpkin or squash weighing about 500g will do.

fondue-filled baby pumpkins

Pumpkins

4 x 500g pumpkins or squashes
1 heaped teaspoon cornflour
2 tablespoons kirsch or white wine
150ml double cream
sea salt, black pepper
freshly grated nutmeg
225g grated Emmental
225g grated Gruyère

Croutons

4 x 1cm slices day-old white bread,
   crusts removed and diced
extra virgin olive oil
a pinch of dried oregano
   or other dried herb

Serves 4

Preheat the oven to 180°C fan/200°C/gas mark 6. Cut the tops off the pumpkins and scoop out the seeds, and if necessary cut a small slice off the bottom so they sit firmly when placed upright, without tipping over. Blend the cornflour with the kirsch or wine, then stir this into the cream and season with salt, pepper and nutmeg. Blend this with the grated cheese in a large bowl and use to fill the pumpkins by about two-thirds. Replace the lids, set them inside a baking or roasting dish and bake for 45 minutes.

In the meantime, scatter the diced bread over the base of a roasting tray, drizzle over a little olive oil and toss with your hands to lightly coat. Scatter over a little oregano and toast in the oven for 8–10 minutes, until lightly golden.

Remove the lids from the cooked pumpkins, spoon off any butter on the surface and give the fondue a stir. Pile the croutons into the centre and serve straight away, spooning the pumpkin flesh away from the skin and eating it with the fondue.

A clafoutis is classically a sweet pudding set with black cherries or prunes. But ultimately it's just a batter pud, and the ingredients are the same as for toad-in-the-hole or Yorkshire pudding, and therefore there is no reason why we cannot borrow and set it with savoury treasures like strips of grilled courgette and nibs of bacon. It easily translates to a vegetarian main course by adding diced medium-mature goat's cheese in lieu of the sautéed bacon.

courgette, smoky bacon and rosemary clafoutis

Batter

110g plain flour, sifted
½ teaspoon sea salt
2 medium eggs
150ml milk
150ml water
2 teaspoons Dijon mustard
2 teaspoons wholegrain mustard

Filling

3 courgettes, ends trimmed,
   sliced lengthways
extra virgin olive oil
sea salt, black pepper
200g rindless smoked streaky
   bacon, diced
1 tablespoon finely chopped
   fresh rosemary

Serves 4

Whiz all the ingredients for the batter together in a blender until smooth, then leave to rest for 30 minutes.

In the meantime, heat a ridged griddle over a medium heat. Brush one side of the courgette slices with oil, season and grill for about 3 minutes until lightly coloured. Brush the top side with oil, turn, and grill this side for about 2 minutes. They need to colour, without being too dark, since they will colour further in the oven. You will probably need to cook them in batches.

Also while the batter is resting, heat a large frying pan over a medium heat, and add the bacon. Fry for 7–8 minutes, stirring occasionally, until lightly coloured and again not too dark, then remove the pan from the heat.

Halfway through resting the batter, preheat the oven to 200°C fan/220°C/gas mark 7. Place a couple of tablespoons of oil in a 30cm oval gratin dish or other dish of a similar size, and heat this in the oven for 10 minutes. Pour the batter into a bowl and stir in the rosemary and half the bacon. Pour this into the dish, then scatter over the courgette slices, pushing down so about half of them are submerged. Scatter over the remaining bacon, and bake for 30 minutes, until the batter is risen and golden. Serve straight away.

It is easy enough to see why the Italians go overboard about this dark green bubbly cabbage, which has a really elegant depth to it. Unlike other cabbages, however, even the finest stalks remain stringy on cooking, so it is important to strip the leaves off them completely.

orecchiette with cavolo nero and chicken livers

approx. 800g cavolo nero
300g orecchiette
2–3 tablespoons extra virgin olive oil
4 garlic cloves, peeled and
    finely chopped
sea salt, black pepper
a pinch of dried chilli flakes
150g freshly grated Parmesan, plus
    extra to serve
300g chicken livers, membranes
    removed, lobes halved if large

Serves 4

Strip the leafy parts of the cavolo nero off the stalks, right up to the tips. Slice the leaves across about 2cm thick and wash.

Bring two large pans of salted water to the boil. Add the cavolo nero to one, cover and simmer for 3 minutes, then drain into a colander and press out any excess water – a potato masher is good for this. Add the orecchiette to the other pan and simmer for 12–14 minutes or according to the packet instructions until just tender. Drain the orecchiette, but not too dry, reserving half a teacup of cooking water, and return the pasta to the saucepan.

Five minutes before the end of cooking the pasta, heat 2 tablespoons of oil in a large frying pan over a medium heat, add the garlic and fry briefly until fragrant and just starting to colour, then add the drained cavolo nero, season with salt and the chilli flakes and fry for a couple of minutes, turning occasionally.

Mix the cavolo nero into the drained pasta. Add the Parmesan, a little seasoning and a drop of the reserved cooking water and heat, turning it now and again, until it appears coated in a creamy emulsion. You can add a little more water if necessary.

Heat a drop of oil in a clean frying pan over a high heat, add the chicken livers, season and sear briefly each side, leaving them pink and creamy in the centre. Mix them into the pasta and accompany with more Parmesan.

gorgeous grains

Grains are only just beginning to reveal the full extent of their talents in the kitchen. For years they've been boxed into a corner, as starchy asides to rib-sticking stews; pearl barley and its type are rarely sold with more advice than 'good in soups' on the packet, when like most other grains they are good for so much more. Lightly dressed with a vinaigrette, with perhaps some sliced mushrooms and chopped dill, toasted pumpkin and sunflower seeds, or shredded leaves, green beans and mint, grains redefine our take on the carbohydrate element within a meal. Most will also make fab risottos.

Spelt is one of the great underrated grains – gorgeously smooth and plump when cooked, it can be used in exactly the same way as barley. Confusingly it is often equated with farro, but cooks up very differently. While farro requires soaking and always remains firm and chewy, spelt can be cooked like rice and turns creamy and yielding by comparison (which is all very convenient for the time-challenged amongst us). It's lovely stuff that laps up the juices of roasted vegetables, for serving warm or as a salad when the two are newly cooled.

Quinoa is another favourite, one that wholly deserves to become the next big thing, yet it sits on the fringes of mainstream cookery. These tiny buff-coloured discs the size of a couscous grain have a really deep, satisfyingly bitter and nutty savour, and a texture quite unlike any other, courtesy of the fine C-shaped tail or germ that separates out from the seed when it cooks. Firmer than couscous, it is still exquisitely delicate. It is in fact a pseudograin, the edible seeds of a species of goosefoot, and not a grass at all. But just as we treat avocados and tomatoes as vegetables rather than fruits, so too quinoa has joined the grain gang in the kitchen.

Spelt, like pearl barley, makes for the most warming and nourishing of hearty soups. It relishes the likes of bacon and cabbage, and a shower of Parmesan added at the end.

wintery spelt soup

2 tomatoes

2 tablespoons extra virgin olive oil

150g rindless unsmoked pancetta
   or streaky bacon, diced

3 garlic cloves, peeled and finely
   chopped

1 teaspoon finely sliced
   medium-hot red chilli

120g pearled spelt, rinsed

1.1 litres chicken or vegetable stock

½ small Savoy cabbage (approx.
   300g), cut into wide strips, tough
   white parts discarded

6 tablespoons coarsely chopped fresh
   flat-leaf parsley, plus extra to serve

sea salt

freshly grated Parmesan to serve

Serves 4

Bring a large pan of water to the boil. Cut out a cone from the top of each tomato, dunk them into the boiling water for about 20 seconds, and then into cold water. Slip off the skins and chop the flesh.

Heat the olive oil in a large saucepan over a medium heat. Add the pancetta or bacon and fry for 5–8 minutes until lightly golden, stirring occasionally, then add the garlic and chilli and cook for a minute longer until fragrant. Add the chopped tomatoes and cook for a few minutes longer until mushy, then stir in the spelt. Add the stock, bring to the boil and simmer for 20 minutes, adding the cabbage after 15 minutes. Stir in the parsley and taste for salt. Serve with extra parsley scattered over, accompanied by Parmesan.

There are few better ways of enjoying the first peas of the summer. Though given the brevity of the season, ready-shelled peas will make a fine stand-in for shell-on peas at any other time. This is half soup, half risotto, and all the stock is added in one go so there's no hanging around the stove.

venetian peas and rice

50g unsalted butter

1 small onion, peeled and chopped

275g fresh shelled peas

200g risotto rice

150ml white wine

1 litre fresh vegetable stock

sea salt, black pepper

70g freshly grated Parmesan

4 tablespoons coarsely chopped fresh
   flat-leaf parsley, plus extra to serve

Serves 4

Heat the butter and onion in a large saucepan and cook until the onion is lightly coloured. Add the peas and rice and stir for a minute or two. Now add the wine, stock and seasoning, bring to a simmer, cover and cook for 15 minutes, by which time the rice should be tender. Stir in the Parmesan and 4 tablespoons of parsley and adjust the seasoning. Scatter each bowl with a little extra parsley and serve straight away, although this is more accommodating than a risotto and will sit around for a few minutes if you're not quite ready to eat.

Delicious dished up with a spicy chutney or syrupy balsamic onions, and die-hard meat-lovers could stir in some little nibs of chorizo (allow about 150g).

bulgar wheat, cashew nut and rocket pilaf

3 tablespoons extra virgin olive oil

1 large onion, peeled and chopped

1 teaspoon ground cumin

1 teaspoon ground coriander

a pinch of dried chilli flakes

3 garlic cloves, peeled and finely chopped

3 strips lemon zest (removed
  with a potato peeler)

1 tablespoon fresh thyme leaves

1 bay leaf

350g bulgar wheat

150ml white wine

500ml fresh chicken or vegetable stock

sea salt

180g rocket, leaves cut in half

125g roasted cashews

soured cream to serve

Serves 6

Heat the olive oil in a medium saucepan over a medium heat. Add the onion and fry for 5–8 minutes until lightly coloured, stirring occasionally. Add the spices, garlic, lemon zest and herbs, give everything a stir and cook for 1 minute longer. Add the bulgar wheat and give it a stir, then add the wine, stock and some salt, bring to the boil and simmer over a low heat for 8 minutes. Remove from the heat, cover and leave to stand for 20 minutes. Discard the bay leaf and lemon zest, add the rocket and cashews and toss. Serve with soured cream.

Butternut squash cooks up like pumpkin but is denser and sweeter, and has the edge in a risotto where it holds its shape. It goes so well with sage, it is hard to deviate to any other herb.

butternut squash and sage risotto

2 tablespoons extra virgin olive oil

1 x 700g butternut squash, skin and seeds removed, thickly sliced

sea salt, black pepper

1.2 litres fresh chicken or vegetable stock

100g unsalted butter

1 onion, peeled and finely chopped

2 garlic cloves, peeled and finely chopped

300g risotto rice

150ml white wine

100g freshly grated Parmesan

a large handful of fresh sage leaves

Serves 4

Heat the olive oil in a large frying pan over a medium heat. Add enough squash to cover the base of the pan (you will probably need to do this in two goes), season and colour on either side.

Bring the stock to the boil in a small saucepan with some seasoning, and keep it at a simmer at the back of the stove, half covered with a lid. Heat half the butter in a medium heavy-bottomed saucepan over a medium heat and sweat the onion and garlic for several minutes, until glossy and relaxed. Add the rice and stir for a minute or two until it is translucent and coated in butter. Add the wine, and once this has been absorbed add the squash and give everything a good stir. Now start to add the stock a few ladles at a time – the rice should be just covered but not flooded. The risotto should take 20–25 minutes to cook once you start to add the liquid, and by the end the squash should be tender. Remove the pan from the heat while the grains still have some resistance, leaving it on the sloppy side. Stir in the Parmesan and taste for seasoning.

Just before the risotto is ready, melt the remaining butter in a medium frying pan over a medium heat. Once the foam subsides, add the sage leaves and fry for a few minutes until pale and crisp. Serve the risotto on warm plates, with the sage leaves and butter spooned over.

Baby leeks have all the flavour you might want from the mature vegetable but with a more delicate texture. This opens all sorts of doors when serving them: salads for instance, or lightly blanched as a little end garnish.

oven-baked saffron risotto with spring veg

Risotto

1 litre chicken or vegetable stock

50g unsalted butter

1 onion, peeled and finely chopped

300g risotto rice

150ml white wine

a pinch of saffron filaments (approx. 20), ground and blended with 1 tablespoon boiling water

sea salt, black pepper

100g freshly grated Parmesan, plus extra to serve

On Top

6 slices of Parma or other air-dried ham, halved lengthways

15g unsalted butter

½ teaspoon caster sugar

6 baby leeks, trimmed and sliced diagonally into 1–2cm pieces

150g fresh shelled peas

150g mangetouts, tops trimmed

Serves 4

Preheat the oven to 170°C fan/190°C/gas mark 5. Bring the stock to the boil in a small saucepan. Melt half the butter in a medium cast iron casserole over a medium heat and fry the onion for a few minutes until translucent. Stir in the rice and cook for 1–2 minutes, stirring occasionally. Add the wine and continue to cook until absorbed, then add the saffron liquid, the stock and plenty of seasoning. Bring to the boil, cover and cook in the oven for 25 minutes.

In the meantime, heat the grill, lay the Parma ham on a grill pan and cook until the fat starts to buckle and appear crisp. This happens quite quickly, so keep an eye on it. Turn and cook the other side.

Ten minutes before the risotto is ready, bring 150ml of water to the boil in a small saucepan over a medium heat with the butter, sugar and ½ teaspoon of salt. Add the leeks, cover and cook for 2 minutes, then stir in the peas and mangetouts, cover and cook for another 2–4 minutes, until the vegetables are just tender. Drain them into a sieve.

Stir the remaining butter and 100g Parmesan into the risotto. It should be a lovely thick dropping consistency, but if necessary you can stir in a tad more hot stock. Serve with the vegetables spooned on top, a little extra Parmesan scattered over, and the grilled ham.

This oven-baked risotto is wonderfully luxurious, with no stinting on the butter; laced with capers, it melts over the scallops at the end. Should you be fortunate enough to find scallops with their corals attached, around twelve should do you. To prepare them, pull the coral away from the meat and with it the surrounding girdle and white gristle (cut off and discard these). Depending on the size of your oven, you will probably need to roast the onions in advance of cooking the risotto.

oven-baked roast onion risotto with scallops

700g red onions, peeled, halved
   and thickly sliced
extra virgin olive oil
sea salt, black pepper
50g unsalted butter, softened
2 garlic cloves, peeled and crushed
   to a paste
300g risotto rice
150ml white wine
1.2 litres chicken or vegetable stock
1 heaped tablespoon capers
3 tablespoons coarsely chopped
   fresh flat-leaf parsley
½ teaspoon finely grated lemon zest,
   plus a squeeze of juice
16 large scallops
100g freshly grated Parmesan

Serves 4

Preheat the oven to 180°C /200°C/gas mark 6. Scatter the onion slices over the base of one or two roasting dishes in a crowded single layer, drizzle over 3 tablespoons of olive oil, season with a little salt and roast for 30–45 minutes until golden, stirring halfway through. Set aside.

Melt half the butter in a large cast-iron casserole over a medium heat, add the garlic and stir until you get a heady hit of garlic butter. Add the rice and stir for about 1 minute, then pour in the wine and simmer until almost completely absorbed. Pour in the stock and season, bring to the boil, cover and cook in the oven for 25 minutes. In the meantime blend the remaining butter with the capers, parsley, lemon zest and juice.

About 10 minutes before the risotto is ready, heat a large non-stick frying pan over a high heat. Toss the scallops with oil to coat them, then season and sear for 1–1½ minutes each side until caramelised; they should give slightly when you press them. You will need to cook them in two batches.

Stir the Parmesan and onions into the rice, and top with the scallops. Pop the remaining butter into the scallop pan and once it appears semi-melted spoon this over the risotto and serve straight away.

Cultivated in the Andes for over 6,000 years, the Incas referred to quinoa as 'the mother of all grains'. And well they might, since it contains more protein than any other grain, and unlike wheat and rice can boast all the essential amino acids, and is gluten-free.

It stands in for bulgar to make a fine tabbouleh, perfect mid-summer when tomatoes are at their best; you could use any that promise to be really sweet and juicy. Try to buy your herbs in nice big bunches, and use just the tender young leaves.

quinoa, feta and herb salad

200g quinoa

3 tablespoons lemon juice

sea salt, black pepper

8 tablespoons extra virgin olive oil

15g young fresh mint leaves,
coarsely chopped

75g young fresh flat-leaf parsley
leaves, coarsely chopped

250g cherry tomatoes, halved
or quartered depending on
their size

6 spring onions, trimmed and
thinly sliced

200g feta, cut into 1cm dice

Serves 4–6

Bring a medium pan of salted water to the boil. Heat a large frying pan over a medium heat, scatter the quinoa over the base and toast for a few minutes, stirring frequently, until it gives off a lovely warming aroma and starts popping. Transfer to a bowl and leave to cool for a few minutes, then add to the boiling water and simmer for 15–20 minutes until tender. Drain into a sieve, return it to the saucepan, cover and leave to cool.

Whisk the lemon juice with 2 tablespoons of water and some seasoning in a small bowl, then whisk in the oil. Combine the herbs in a large bowl with the tomatoes, spring onions and cooled quinoa. You can prepare the salad to this point up to a couple of hours in advance. Shortly before serving add the dressing and toss, then gently mix in the feta.

This salad just sings with goodness. I love to toss tart sweet fruits into tabbouleh – mango slivers, redcurrants or pomegranate seeds, as well as grapes. As with the salad on page 105, your parsley needs to be young and tender, so avoid any overgrown bunches. Should you have any tabbouleh left over, seal the surface with a lettuce leaf and cover with clingfilm.

tabbouleh with grapes

1½ tablespoons fine bulgar*
100g fresh flat-leaf parsley,
    tough stalks removed
2 tomatoes, sliced and then chopped
a handful of fresh mint leaves, chopped
1 large spring onion, finely sliced
    and then chopped
sea salt, black pepper
3 tablespoons extra virgin olive oil
2 tablespoons lemon juice
75g each of red and white seedless (or
    seeded) grapes, halved

Serves 4

Rinse the bulgar in a fine-mesh sieve and leave it on the side to absorb the remaining moisture. Chop the parsley, starting at the leaf end and working towards the stalk. Combine the parsley, tomatoes, mint and onion in a bowl, then add some seasoning, olive oil and lemon juice and combine. Mix in the bulgar and the grapes, reserving a few to scatter over at the end, then pile the salad on to a plate or dish.

*Fine bulgar is available from Middle Eastern delis. Alternatively whiz ordinary bulgar wheat in a coffee grinder until about half the size.

Red rice is lovely stuff – nutty and aromatic, it lends itself more readily to salads than white rice. This serves as an aside within a selection of salads, perhaps to some grilled chicken escalopes or other small tasty cut.

red rice salad

250g red rice
2 tablespoons lemon juice
4 tablespoons extra virgin olive oil
2 tablespoons finely chopped shallots
8 tablespoons mixed finely chopped
   fresh flat-leaf parsley, mint, basil
   and dill
sea salt, black pepper

Serves 4–6

Bring a large pan of salted water to the boil. Add the rice and simmer for 30–35 minutes until tender, then drain into a sieve or colander and run cold water through it. Toss the rice in a bowl with the lemon juice, olive oil, shallots, herbs and some seasoning.

A dollop of garlicky yoghurt provides a little luxury – blend 200g of Greek yoghurt with a crushed small garlic clove or two, a little salt and a pinch of sugar. It strikes just the right note alongside a joint of rare seared beef or lamb too.

couscous with green beans, mint and lemon

sea salt

5 tablespoons extra virgin olive oil

300g couscous

200g fine French beans,
   stalk ends removed

200g sugar snaps, stalk ends
   removed

2 tablespoons lemon juice

a handful of fresh mint leaves, torn

2 tablespoons finely diced
   preserved lemon

Serves 6

Bring a large pan of salted water to the boil for the beans. At the same time bring 450ml water to the boil in a medium saucepan with a little salt and 1 tablespoon of oil. Add the couscous and simmer for 1 minute. Cover with a tightly fitting lid and leave to stand for 10 minutes.

Halfway into this time add the beans to the large pan of boiling water, cook for 2 minutes, then add the sugar snaps and cook for another 2 minutes. Drain into a sieve and leave for a few minutes for the surface moisture to evaporate.

Fluff up the couscous with a fork, then mix in the beans and sugar snaps. Blend the lemon juice with a little salt, add the remaining oil and pour this dressing over the couscous. Serve scattered with the torn mint and the preserved lemon. This salad can be served warm or cold.

Spelt laps up the juices from roasted peppers, but butternut squash roasted with cherry tomatoes and lots of red onions is another mélange that would welcome the grain. Cooked spelt is extraordinarily good-natured, and unlike most grains that continue to absorb a salad dressing once it's mixed in, this is in much the same condition the day after you make it. It's worth, though, holding back on tossing in the basil leaves until close to the time of serving, to ensure they remain suitably perky.

roasted pepper, spelt and pistachio salad

7 long red peppers, core and seeds removed, halved lengthways and cut into wide strips

1 medium-hot red chilli, core and seeds removed, cut into long thin strips

7 tablespoons extra virgin olive oil

sea salt

3 red onions, peeled, halved and thickly sliced

4 garlic cloves, peeled and sliced

2 tablespoons balsamic vinegar

200g pearled spelt

a handful of fresh basil leaves, torn

30g shelled pistachio nuts

Serves 6

Preheat the oven to 200°C fan/220°C/gas mark 7. Arrange the peppers and chilli strips in a crowded single layer in a roasting dish. Drizzle over 4 tablespoons of olive oil and season with salt. Roast for 40–50 minutes, stirring in the onions after 20 minutes, and the garlic after 30 minutes. Everything should be nicely golden at the edges by the end. When the peppers come out of the oven, drizzle over the vinegar and remaining olive oil and leave to cool.

At the same time bring a large pan of salted water to the boil, add the spelt and simmer for 15–20 minutes until just tender. Drain into a sieve, then return it to the pan, cover and leave to cool.

Mix the spelt into the peppers and onions, and add the basil and pistachios.

Inspiration for this comes from UP or Urban Picnic, a boutique lunch take-out in East London – they complete this particular line-up of salads with roast or barbecued butterflied lamb rubbed with sumac.

barley salad with honeyed tomatoes and dates

Barley Salad

120g pearl barley

1 teaspoon coriander seeds

½ tablespoon red wine vinegar

sea salt, black pepper

4 tablespoons extra virgin olive oil

50g pitted black olives, halved
   lengthways

a few handfuls of rocket leaves

Courgettes

2 courgettes, ends removed, cut into
   long thin strips

extra virgin olive oil

Tomato Salad

2 teaspoons runny honey

1 tablespoon lemon juice

3 tablespoons extra virgin olive oil

200g cocktail plum tomatoes, e.g.
   Marzinino, quartered lengthways

100g Medjool dates, stoned and
   quartered lengthways

Serves 4

Bring a large pan of salted water to the boil, add the barley and simmer for 40–45 minutes or until tender. Drain into a sieve, return to the saucepan, cover and leave to cool.

Heat a small frying pan over a medium heat and briefly toast the coriander seeds, then coarsely grind them using a pestle and mortar. Whisk the vinegar with some seasoning, then whisk in the oil and stir in the coriander. Toss the barley with the dressing and mix in the olives. You can prepare the salad to this point several hours in advance.

Heat a ridged griddle over a medium-high heat. Take as many courgette slices as will fit the griddle, brush them with olive oil on one side and season. Grill this side for 3–5 minutes until striped with gold, then brush the other side with oil, turn and grill this side too. Remove them to a plate and grill the remainder in the same fashion. Leave the slices to cool – you can cook them well in advance.

Whisk the honey, lemon juice and some seasoning in a small bowl, then whisk in the oil. Toss with the tomatoes and dates in a bowl.

Toss in the rocket just before eating and serve with the grilled courgettes and tomato salad.

potatoes

Little is more comforting in times of trouble than a thick potato soup. And it has to be maincrop for this, their loose mealy consistency is ideal for melting into a rich stock. This wholesome leek and potato soup is one of the backbones of my kitchen, that I make by the large panful whenever anyone in the family is feeling below par. While sweet potatoes that cook to a beautiful melting softness make for a deliciously aromatic and velvety soup that's just as soothing.

We are rarely starved of waxy-fleshed or 'new' potatoes these days, even in the midst of winter, which makes potato salads a year-round treat. But there is no beating the summer crop of first earlies that includes Jersey Royals, defined by their papery skin that doesn't need peeling so much as tending with a scrubbing brush. The recalcitrant flakes left clinging are a part of their charm and imperceptible in eating. Thicker than this and I do peel them, but not real tinies which would disappear down the sink.

My favourite potato salad contains a mass of freshly chopped tender herbs. Dressed while warm the potatoes actually improve if you leave the salad overnight, something that always appeals to lazy cooks who hate doing everything at the last minute, and is useful if you are planning a barbecue or Sunday lunch. The other magic ingredient for any potato salad is a little onion, added judiciously, and it's stardust. Spring onions are raised for the job, red onions are sweeter and milder than white ones, and finely chopped shallot will fire things up nicely too. But if you want to be really subtle, slip a few drops of onion juice, squeezed through a garlic press, into the dressing instead.

A completely different animal from vichyssoise, mealy, wholesome and nicely slippery. Children of all ages adore this soup, and it's one that I crave when feeling in any way delicate – it nurtures perfectly. It's also good for Sunday night if you've got a pot of homemade chicken stock sitting on the hob; quite likely you will have the other ingredients in house too. The bacon of course isn't *de rigueur*.

leek and potato soup

50g unsalted butter

700g leeks (trimmed weight), sliced

1 large onion, peeled and chopped

200ml white wine

1.3 litres fresh chicken
   or vegetable stock

180g maincrop potatoes,
   peeled and thinly sliced

sea salt, black pepper

200g rindless unsmoked streaky
   bacon, diced

snipped fresh chives

Serves 6

Melt the butter in a large saucepan over a medium-low heat and sweat the leeks and onion for 8–10 minutes, without colouring, until they are silky and soft, stirring them occasionally. Add the wine and reduce until syrupy. Meanwhile bring the stock to the boil in a separate pan. Add the sliced potatoes to the leeks and stir them around for 1 minute, then pour the boiling stock over, season and simmer for 8 minutes.

At the same time, heat a frying pan over a medium low heat, add the bacon, and fry for 7–8 minutes, until it is dark and crisp, stirring occasionally. Transfer it to a bowl with a slotted spoon.

Blitz the soup in batches in a food processor to a textured slurry. Return it to a clean saucepan, taste to check the seasoning and gently reheat. Ladle the soup into warm bowls, scatter over the bacon and chives and serve.

As thick, comforting and mealy as you would hope a sweet potato soup to be. And it's the orange-fleshed potatoes you want here rather than the cream-coloured ones. The Roquefort is particularly good with all that sweetness, but it could just as well be shreds of chorizo or little croutons.

sweet potato and rosemary soup

extra virgin olive oil

1 large onion, peeled and chopped

1 heaped tablespoon fresh rosemary
   leaves

4 garlic cloves, peeled and
   finely chopped

a pinch of dried chilli flakes

1kg orange-fleshed sweet potatoes,
   peeled and thickly sliced

1.2 litres fresh chicken or vegetable
   stock

sea salt

60–90g Roquefort, crumbled

Serves 4–6

Heat 3 tablespoons of olive oil in a large saucepan over a medium heat. Add the onion and rosemary and fry for 3–5 minutes until relaxed and glossy, stirring occasionally. Add the garlic and chilli and fry for a minute or two longer. Add the sweet potatoes and continue to cook for another couple of minutes, stirring frequently. Pour in the stock and season with salt, then bring to the boil and simmer over a low heat for 20 minutes, by which time the potato should be meltingly tender. Liquidise the soup in batches and pass through a sieve. Return it to the saucepan and season with a little more salt if necessary. The soup can be prepared well in advance.

Reheat if necessary, and serve in warm bowls. Scatter over the Roquefort – most of this will sink and melt, but a little should peek out at the top. Drizzle over a little olive oil and serve.

There is something very dated about baked potatoes: it was Spudulike that did for their reputation. But they are very tasty, and this James Bond-like preference for 'crushed not mashed' seeks to bring them forward to the present day.

What are sold as baking potatoes are not so much special varieties as potatoes of a particular size – they should be 225–275g in weight. There are usually one or two potatoes in an ordinary pack that will be large enough for baking. These can be filled and then chilled until required and reheated.

crushed not mashed

Potatoes
4 baking or maincrop potatoes, e.g. Maris Piper, Desirée, King Edward
extra virgin olive oil
coarse-grain sea salt, e.g. Maldon

Filling
2 heaped tablespoons coarsely chopped fresh flat-leaf parsley
½ garlic clove, peeled and crushed
sea salt, black pepper

Serves 4

Preheat the oven to 160°C fan/180°C/gas mark 4. Scrub the potatoes and dry them. Make an incision the shape of a lid on the top of each one with a small sharp knife. Pour a little olive oil into the palm of your hand and rub your hands together and then over the potatoes, lightly coating each one with the oil. Place them in a baking dish, sprinkle over some crystals of sea salt, and bake for 1½ hours, until the skin is rich and crisp and the insides are fluffy.

Use a spoon to remove the potato from the skins and roughly crush with a fork. Combine with 5 tablespoons of olive oil, the chopped parsley, garlic and seasoning, and refill.

Sautéd potatoes are the chips of the home, arguably more delicious with all those crispy little nibs, and it's worth cooking them skin-on for this. Butter combined with olive oil gives you the best of both worlds, as you get that lovely flavour without the risk of burning, but you can vary this, and goose fat is always a promise of a fab fry-up. It's worth taking your time – frying the potatoes slowly allows the sugars to caramelise. The fried onions turn them into Lyonnaise potatoes, but you can go on building: fried wild mushrooms, grilled bacon, poached eggs.

lyonnaise potatoes

600g waxy potatoes, e.g. Charlotte
    or La Ratte, scrubbed
25g unsalted butter
3 tablespoons extra virgin olive oil
sea salt, black pepper
1 garlic clove, peeled and finely chopped
2 tablespoons finely chopped fresh
    flat-leaf parsley
2 large onions (ideally white), peeled,
    halved and finely sliced
1 teaspoon red wine vinegar

Serves 3–4

Bring a large pan of salted water to the boil, add the potatoes and cook for 15–20 minutes until tender when pierced with a knife. Drain them into a colander, leave to cool, then slice them thickly.

Heat the butter and 1 tablespoon of olive oil in a large frying pan over a low heat and sauté the potatoes for about 20 minutes, turning them every few minutes or so, until they are evenly golden and crisp, seasoning them a few minutes into cooking. Five minutes towards the end, add the chopped garlic. Finally sprinkle over the chopped parsley and toss to distribute it.

At the same time as frying the potatoes, heat the remaining olive oil in a large frying pan over a low heat, and gently fry the onions for 20–25 minutes, stirring frequently until they are evenly gold and sweet. At the very end, season them with salt, pepper and the red wine vinegar. Toss them into the sautéd potatoes and serve straight away.

Feta tossed into small crispy roast tatties at the end of their cooking time just melts and softens, and the herbs broaden out their appeal. Take advantage of any soft herbs you have growing in the garden, also the pale green leafy fronds on the inside of fennel bulbs or celery hearts. You could just about get away with settling down to a plate of these without a roast in tow, which you would be hard pushed to do with normal roast potatoes. You can peel the potatoes or leave them unpeeled if you prefer, they will be equally good in a rustic fashion.

crispy roasties with feta

1.3kg medium waxy potatoes, peeled or unpeeled, halved lengthways

3 tablespoons extra virgin olive oil

sea salt

200g feta, diced

2 tablespoons coarsely chopped fresh flat-leaf parsley

2 tablespoons snipped fresh chives

Serves 6

Heat the oven to 200°C fan/220°C/gas mark 7. Bring a large pan of salted water to the boil, add the potatoes and cook for 10 minutes. Drain into a colander and leave for a few minutes for the surface moisture to evaporate, then return them to the pan and give them a vigorous shake. Add the olive oil and toss, and season with salt. Tip these into a large roasting dish, so they fit in a crowded single layer. Roast for 1 hour, stirring them halfway through. Stir in the feta and return to the oven for 5 minutes, then scatter over the herbs and serve.

This has lots and lots of fresh herbs in it, and you can use whatever you have growing. The potatoes are dressed warm, and infuse with the lively scents – in fact it's even better left overnight.

a stock favourite potato salad

750g small waxy potatoes, peeled
  or scrubbed

Dressing
2 tablespoons white wine
9 tablespoons extra virgin olive oil
4 tablespoons chopped fresh herbs,
  e.g. parsley, chives, basil,
  chervil, tarragon
2 spring onions, trimmed
  and finely sliced
sea salt, black pepper

Serves 4–6

Lay the potatoes in the top half of a steamer set over a little boiling water in the lower half, cover and cook until tender. Rinse the steamer under the cold tap to wash off the sticky starch on the surface of the potatoes. Alternatively bring a large pan of salted water to the boil, add the potatoes, cook for 15–20 minutes until tender when a skewer is inserted, then drain into a colander.

Thickly slice the hot potatoes, place in a bowl and pour over the wine and olive oil. Gently toss in the herbs, spring onions and some seasoning. Leave to cool to room temperature. If not serving straight away, cover and chill. In this case bring back up to room temperature for 30 minutes before serving.

The iodine-rich flavour of anchovies is gracefully absorbed by the sweetness of the potatoes. With slivers of red onion in there too, this is quite a bold potato salad, and as ever with anchovies the mind strays to tomatoes and olives, or even some lightly cooked eggs.

potato, anchovy and red onion salad

1kg medium waxy potatoes,
    peeled and halved if large
9 tablespoons extra virgin olive oil
1 tablespoon lemon juice
sea salt, black pepper
8 anchovy fillets, thinly sliced across
1 red onion, peeled, halved
    and thinly sliced
4 tablespoons coarsely chopped
    fresh flat-leaf parsley

Serves 4

Bring a large pan of salted water to the boil, add the potatoes and simmer for 15–20 minutes until tender when a skewer is inserted. Drain them into a colander and leave to cool for about 10 minutes. Halve or quarter them depending on their size and place in a large bowl. Pour over the olive oil and lemon juice and season them, then fold in the remaining ingredients. Leave the salad to cool completely.

This can also be made a day in advance, covered and chilled, in which case fold in the parsley just before serving, and bring back up to room temperature for 30 minutes before eating.

potato salad with roquefort and walnuts

Salad

750g small waxy potatoes, peeled
  or scrubbed

90g walnut halves

1 large or 2 small heads of chicory

1 celery heart, outer sticks discarded
  and finely sliced

2 spring onions, trimmed and thinly
  sliced

200g Roquefort

40g watercress sprigs

Dressing

1 tablespoon red wine vinegar

a squeeze of lemon juice

1 scant teaspoon Dijon mustard

sea salt, black pepper

4 tablespoons walnut oil

4 tablespoons groundnut oil

Serves 4–6

Lay the potatoes in the top half of a steamer set over a little boiling water in the lower half, cover and cook until tender. Rinse the steamer under the cold tap to wash off the sticky starch on the surface of the potatoes. Alternatively bring a large pan of salted water to the boil, add the potatoes, cook for 15–20 minutes until tender when a skewer is inserted, then drain into a colander. Leave the potatoes to cool while you assemble the remaining ingredients.

Roughly break the walnut halves into 2 or 3 pieces. Heat a frying pan over a medium heat and toast them for 3 minutes, tossing constantly to ensure they don't burn. Transfer them to a bowl or plate and leave to cool. Trim the base of the chicory bulbs and remove the outer leaves. Halve them, cut out the inner core and slice into long thin strips. Whisk the vinegar and lemon juice in a small bowl with the mustard and some seasoning, then whisk in the oils.

Place the potatoes in a large bowl, pour over the dressing and gently turn to coat them. Now mix in the celery, spring onions, chicory and walnuts. Using your fingers, crumble the Roquefort into cubes about 1cm in size and gently fold them into the salad to avoid mushing them up. Finally toss in the watercress. Pile the salad on to a large serving dish, or individual plates.

Colour is everything here: the potatoes are dyed a sunny gold by the saffron. They should be big enough to peel without disappearing, but small enough to leave whole. And as ever, unless you are using very young broad beans that can be eaten skin and all, frozen baby ones might be a better bet, otherwise it's best to peel them.

saffron potato and bean salad

¼ teaspoon saffron filaments, ground
800g small waxy potatoes
200g baby broad beans
150g sugar snaps, stalk ends removed
2 tablespoons white wine
9 tablespoons extra virgin olive oil
sea salt, black pepper
a couple of squeezes of lemon juice
4 tablespoons coarsely chopped fresh flat-leaf parsley

Serves 6–8

Bring just enough salted water to cover the potatoes to the boil in a medium saucepan. Add a little boiling water to the ground saffron, pour the liquor into the pan and give the water a stir. Add the potatoes and simmer for 15–20 minutes until tender. Drain them into a colander and leave for a few minutes for the surface water to evaporate.

Bring another two medium pans of water to the boil. Add the broad beans to one and simmer for 4–6 minutes, until tender, then drain them into a sieve and briefly run cold water through them. Add the sugar snaps to the other pan, cook for 1 minute, then drain and run cold water through those as well.

Place the warm potatoes in a large bowl and dress with the wine, olive oil and some seasoning. Toss in the broad beans and sugar snaps. Add a couple of squeezes of lemon juice and leave to cool. Toss in the parsley. If not serving within a couple of hours, cover and chill until required, and bring back to room temperature for 1 hour before eating, adding the lemon juice at the last minute.

Chips don't have to be deep-fried to taste good, it's inherent in their shape, and if you boil chipped potatoes and dress them with a vinaigrette they're pretty good too. So this is a variation on the theme of fish and chips. Any seafood that is good eaten cold can be included – cooked mussels, clams or squid. Vary the choice according to availability. I like to use nice juicy prawns, with their tail fans attached. Should your scallops come 'coral-less', then up the number to nine or ten.

fish and chip salad

600g medium waxy potatoes,
    scrubbed or peeled
6 large scallops
6 tablespoons extra virgin olive oil
250g cooked prawns
3 tablespoons caper berries, rinsed
    and stalks removed
4 tablespoons coarsely chopped
    fresh flat-leaf parsley
1 tablespoon lemon juice
sea salt

Serves 4

Bring a medium pan of salted water to the boil. Cut the potatoes into 1cm chips, boil for about 10 minutes until tender, then carefully drain them into a sieve and leave to cool.

Separate the corals from the scallop meat, pulling off the gristle and skirt with them. Cut off and discard the gristle and slice the scallop meat into thin discs. Heat 1 tablespoon of oil in a large frying pan over a high heat, add the scallop discs and corals and cook for about 30 seconds each side until they turn opaque. Transfer them to a large bowl and leave to cool.

Add the prawns, caper berries, parsley, the remaining olive oil, lemon juice, and a little salt to the scallops and toss, then gently mix in the potatoes.

big salads

It's as though every decade of late has left a legacy in salads. The Sixties were all about floppy lettuces and salad cream, still a winner when the leaves are carefully prepared and crisped in ice-cold water, and the salad cream is homemade with English mustard and plenty of sugar. The Seventies were a bit bald, mind you, it was all rather hale and hearty, while in the Eighties things became a little more interesting, with 'warm salads' that bridged the divide between a side salad and a main course – the tender breast of a quail gently wilting a mound of escarole, or the yolk of a lightly poached egg trickling down. And the Nineties was shaped by our love affair with all things Italian, those gorgeous roasted vegetables (see page 24) that we are still avidly pursuing.

Today, however, is all about 'BIG' salads, overstated splashes of Renaissance exuberance and colour, with all restraint banished. The emphasis, quite rightly, is on allure. I have to fight fingers out of the salad bowl to make sure it is not denuded of crisp snippets of bacon and toasted pine nuts before it reaches the table. Nuts toasted to a crisp, caper berries and raisins build interest into the equation. I also love that mix of cooked and raw, some leaves thrown in with blanched mangetouts and peas, and sharp accents, like lemon and mint added to slippery fried courgettes. It's as though salads are going through a rather lovely hippy phase.

One or two of these, prepared well in advance, sitting on the table, and whatever else you choose to dish up with them is a doddle. You can turn to the barbecue, chuck a rib of beef or shoulder of lamb into the oven, or more modestly fry up some sardines or other fish fillets with the simplest marinade – equal quantities of lemon juice and olive oil, some crushed fennel seeds and a little cayenne pepper is a favourite in our house.

If cauliflower was a different shape then I'm sure we'd be griddling away and eating rather more of it in salads than we do. Still, it works well providing it has a few sparring partners, like pickles and chillies. But don't be tempted to use two small chillies instead of one large one – their size is in inverse ratio to their heat, and you want a nice spicy nip rather than full on hit.

cauliflower, mangetouts, chilli and caper berry salad

1 cauliflower, cut into 2–3cm florets
  (approx. 700g)
250g mangetouts, stalk ends trimmed
1½ tablespoons red wine vinegar
1 heaped teaspoon Dijon mustard
1 heaped teaspoon honey
1 garlic clove, peeled and crushed
  to a paste
sea salt
9 tablespoons extra virgin olive oil
1 large fresh red chilli, seeds
  discarded and cut into fine strips
150g caper berries, stalks removed

Serves 6

Bring a large pan of salted water to the boil, add the cauliflower florets and cook for 6 minutes, then add the mangetouts and cook for another 2 minutes. Drain into a colander, briefly run under the cold tap, then leave to cool.

Transfer the vegetables to a shallow serving dish. Whisk the vinegar, mustard, honey, garlic and some salt together in a small bowl, then add the oil and whisk until you have a thick creamy emulsion. Scatter the chilli strips and caper berries over the salad, drizzle over the dressing and scatter with a little more salt.

The spicy crisp almonds serve as a piquant burst of flavour, hard to resist on their own; they toast up well as a snack at any other time.

spinach, cherry tomato and avocado salad

Nuts

80g whole almonds, skinned
1 tablespoon extra virgin olive oil
1 teaspoon dark soy sauce
1 teaspoon fresh thyme leaves
¼ teaspoon cayenne pepper

Salad

2 avocados
125g baby spinach leaves, or sliced
    young spinach leaves
2 tablespoons extra virgin olive oil
a squeeze of lemon juice
200g cherry tomatoes on the vine,
    halved
a small handful of fresh chives,
    halved
sea salt

Serves 4–6

Preheat the oven to 170°C fan/190°C/gas mark 5. Toss the almonds in a bowl with the olive oil and soy sauce, then toss in the thyme, scatter over the cayenne pepper and toss again. Tip the nuts into a small roasting or baking dish and spread them out in a single layer. Toast in the oven for 15–20 minutes, until deep golden and crisp. Transfer the nuts to a plate and leave to cool.

Remove the avocados from the stone in two halves, and pick the stone out. Halve these again into quarters and peel off the skin, then slice each quarter into two long segments. Toss the spinach in a large bowl with the olive oil and lemon juice, then carefully fold in the cherry tomatoes and avocado. Pile the salad on to plates and scatter over the spiced nuts and chives. Serve straight away, leaving each diner to season their own salad with sea salt.

A wintery mélange: make this around Christmas and you should have the cheeses to go with it, a sliver of something blue and creamy or a flaky mature Cheddar.

salad of red cabbage, apple and dates

Salad

50g hazelnuts, skinned and halved

¼ red cabbage (approx. 250g)

1 apple, cored and thinly sliced

75g Medjool dates, stoned, and
   quartered lengthways

3 spring onions, trimmed and
   finely sliced diagonally

Dressing

1 tablespoon red wine vinegar

1 teaspoon Dijon mustard

1 level teaspoon caster sugar

sea salt, black pepper

3 tablespoons hazelnut oil

3 tablespoons groundnut oil

Serves 4

Preheat the oven to 180°C fan/200°C/gas mark 6. Place the hazelnuts on a small baking tray and toast them for 8–10 minutes, until lightly golden. Remove and leave to cool. Slice the red cabbage as finely as possible, then halve the strands and discard any tough white ones.

Whisk the vinegar with the mustard, sugar and some salt and pepper, then whisk in the oils until you have a creamy emulsified dressing. Toss the red cabbage, apple, dates and spring onions in a bowl. You can do this a couple of hours in advance of eating, in which case cover and set aside. Shortly before serving, mix in half the nuts, rewhisk the dressing if necessary and drizzle it over, then scatter over the rest of the nuts.

Organic and healthfood shops with a fresh vegetable section tend to be the best source for sprouting seeds. Mung beans are particularly good should you chance upon them.

mixed sprouts with spinach and toasted almonds

Nuts

80g whole almonds, unskinned

1 tablespoon groundnut oil

1 teaspoon dark soy sauce

¼ teaspoon cayenne pepper

Salad

150g mung bean or mixed sprouts

75g alfalfa sprouts

extra virgin olive oil

1 tablespoon lemon juice

sea salt, black pepper

a few handfuls of young spinach leaves

Serves 4

Preheat the oven to 170°C fan/190°C/gas mark 5. Toss the almonds in a bowl with the oil and soy sauce, then dust with the cayenne pepper and toss again. Tip the nuts into a small roasting or baking dish and spread them out in a single layer. Toast in the oven for 15–20 minutes, until deep golden and crisp. Transfer the nuts to a plate and leave to cool.

Place the mung bean or mixed sprouts and the alfalfa in a bowl and combine, teasing the alfalfa apart. Drizzle over 2 tablespoons of olive oil and ¾ tablespoon of lemon juice, season and toss. Toss the spinach leaves in another bowl with a dash more oil, a squeeze of lemon and a little seasoning. Divide the spinach between four plates and pile the sprouts on top. Scatter over the almonds and serve.

There's nothing challenging in the way of textures here – the fried courgettes are as meltingly tender as the buffalo mozzarella, but given a little jolt by the mint and lemon.

salad of mozzarella, courgettes, lemon and mint

extra virgin olive oil

4 medium courgettes, ends
   trimmed, sliced diagonally

sea salt, black pepper

2 buffalo mozzarellas, sliced

2 tablespoons fresh mint leaves

2 tablespoons lemon juice

Serves 4

You will probably need to cook the courgettes in two or three goes to avoid overcrowding the pan. Heat 2 tablespoons of olive oil in a large frying pan over a medium heat, add some of the courgettes, season and fry them for 4–5 minutes, turning them frequently, until translucent and starting to colour, but remaining crisp. Don't worry if they haven't coloured evenly.

Transfer them to a shallow serving dish (I use a 35cm oval gratin dish), and cook the remainder in the same fashion, adding more oil to the pan as necessary. Leave the courgettes to cool. You can cook them several hours in advance, in which case cover and set aside in a cool place.

To finish assembling the salad, season the courgettes with a little more sea salt, then mix in the sliced mozzarella and mint. Whisk the lemon juice with 4 tablespoons of olive oil and pour it over. Try to serve within 30–60 minutes.

The lightly boiled eggs and slivers of Parmesan turn this into a slightly more substantial salad that will serve as a starter or light lunch, but if you're serving it as one of a selection of salads or as an accompaniment you can leave them out.

salad of green beans with caper berries and parmesan

300g fine green beans, stalk ends
  trimmed
200g mangetouts, stalk ends trimmed
4 medium eggs
4 purple (or green) spring onions,
  trimmed and thinly sliced diagonally
6 tablespoons extra virgin olive oil
sea salt, black pepper
75g caper berries, stalks removed
50g finely shaved Parmesan

Serves 4

Bring a large pan of salted water to the boil, add the green beans and cook for 4 minutes, adding the mangetouts after 2 minutes. Drain the vegetables into a colander, briefly run cold water through them to halt the cooking process and set aside to cool.

In the meantime, bring a small pan of water to the boil and cook the eggs for 6 minutes. Drain them, then run cold water into the pan and leave to cool completely.

Toss the beans, mangetouts and spring onions with the olive oil in a bowl. (You can prepare the salad to this point in advance.) Shortly before serving season the salad and toss in the caper berries. Divide the salad between four plates. Shell and halve the eggs and arrange them on top, then scatter over the Parmesan.

A mélange of close relatives – mangetouts, sugar snaps and peas – that all relish crisp salty bacon nibs. White balsamic vinegar is gentle and sweet, and I grow fonder of it every time I use it, but you can play around with the dressing to suit your storecupboard.

pea, bacon and pine nut salad

200g mangetouts, stalk ends trimmed
200g sugar snaps, stalk ends trimmed
150g fresh shelled peas
200g rindless unsmoked streaky
   bacon, diced
50g pine nuts
5 tablespoons avocado oil
2 tablespoons white balsamic vinegar
sea salt, black pepper
1 tablespoon coarsely chopped
   fresh tarragon
50g lamb's lettuce

Serves 6

Bring a large pan of salted water to the boil. Add the mangetouts, sugar snaps and peas, bring back to the boil and cook for 2 minutes or until tender. Drain them into a colander and refresh under the cold tap, then leave to cool.

Heat a large frying pan over a medium heat. Add the bacon, separating out the pieces, and fry for 4–5 minutes, until half-coloured, stirring frequently. Add the pine nuts and fry for another 2–3 minutes, until both are golden, again stirring frequently. Remove with a slotted spoon to a double thickness of kitchen paper to drain and cool. You can prepare the recipe to this point an hour or two in advance.

Shortly before serving, toss the vegetables with the oil, vinegar, a pinch of salt and some pepper, then fold in the bacon and pine nuts, the tarragon and the lamb's lettuce.

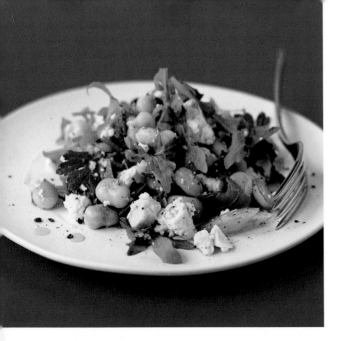

Frozen baby broad beans are one of the best finds in the freezer cabinet. It would take you a long time to amass this number from a mountain of pods, but if it happens to be early enough in the season, before their skins toughen, fresh would be a treat.

broad bean and feta salad

500g frozen baby broad beans
extra virgin olive oil
juice of ½ lemon
sea salt, black pepper
3 spring onions, trimmed
  and finely sliced diagonally
6 tablespoons coarsely chopped
  fresh flat-leaf parsley
200g feta, crumbled
50g rocket leaves (optional)

Serves 4–6

Bring a large pan of water to the boil and cook the broad beans according to the packet instructions. Drain into a colander and leave for a few minutes for the water to evaporate. Toss the hot beans in a bowl with the 6 tablespoons of olive oil, the lemon juice and some seasoning and leave to cool.

Toss in the spring onions and two-thirds of the parsley. Scatter the feta and remaining parsley over the top and splash over a little more oil. The salad is good to eat for some time, but it will absorb the dressing after several hours so you may want to add a little more oil just before serving. You can also toss a few rocket leaves into the salad or serve it scattered over a few dressed leaves.

Both baby romanesco cauliflowers and fennel have an even better texture in their nascent state than when they are larger. Carrots too should be on the thin side in the name of delicacy. The anchovies here could just as well be olives.

caponata of summer vegetables

5 tablespoons extra virgin olive oil

150g each of cauliflower or romanesco
   florets, broccoli florets, young carrots
   (peeled, halved and cut into 3cm
   lengths), yellow or green beans
   (stalk ends trimmed, halved), fennel
   segments or baby fennel (halved)

1 bunch of spring onions, trimmed
   and halved

150ml white wine

sea salt, black pepper

juice of ½ lemon

6 anchovy fillets in oil,
   halved lengthways

2 tablespoons capers, rinsed

3 tablespoons coarsely chopped
   fresh flat-leaf parsley

Serves 4

Heat 2 tablespoons of the olive oil in a large saucepan over a medium heat, then add all the vegetables and sweat for about 5 minutes until they begin to colour, stirring occasionally. Add the wine and some seasoning, cover the pan and cook over a low heat for 5 minutes or until just tender, but with a little resistance. Transfer the vegetables to a bowl and reduce the residual liquor to a couple of tablespoons. Pour this over the vegetables and leave them to cool.

To finish the caponata, pour over the lemon juice and remaining olive oil. Toss in the anchovies, capers and parsley, and taste for seasoning.

This idiosyncratic salad comes from a favourite book, *Real Greek Food*, by Theodore Kyriakou and Charles Campion. It's almost too tempting not to serve some fried halloumi and oily black olives alongside.

salad of green peppers and peaches

900g green peppers

8 tablespoons extra virgin olive oil

1 level tablespoon brown sugar

sea salt, black pepper

3 large ripe (but not over-ripe) peaches
  or nectarines

½ tablespoon cumin seeds

¼ teaspoon cayenne pepper

½ tablespoon lemon juice

Serves 4

Preheat the oven to 170°C fan/190°C/gas mark 5. Remove the core and seeds from the green peppers and quarter them. Arrange them in a roasting dish, drizzle over half the olive oil, scatter over the sugar and season well. Roast for 45–60 minutes, giving them a stir halfway through to ensure they caramelise evenly. Remove and leave to cool.

If you are feeling fastidious you can peel the peaches or nectarines – plunge them into a pan of boiling water for 30 seconds, then into a sink of cold water, and slip off the skins using a knife to assist. Slice them into wedges and slip out the stone. Place the slices in a salad bowl and mix in the green peppers and any juices in the bottom of the pan.

Heat the cumin seeds in a small frying pan over a medium heat until they begin to smell fragrant, tossing them constantly. Crush them using a pestle and mortar, then combine with the cayenne pepper and a little salt, and toss this into the salad. Add the remaining olive oil and lemon juice and toss again. Check the seasoning and serve.

small salads

These salads are united in size, and will play support roles beside whatever small cuts have taken your fancy at the butcher or fishmonger. The lead is a very simple tomato salad, something I tend to make as a matter of course with almost every dinner. I buy tomatoes throughout the week, especially during the summer months, gathering different varieties wherever I'm shopping to top up the 'tomato bowl', which at its best is every bit as showy as the fruit bowl. Like a green salad, a plate of lightly seasoned sliced tomatoes has the ability to go with pretty much whatever you serve it with. It's that balance of sweet and sour that always seem to provide the missing note, and get along with everything.

Coleslaw is another classic favourite, delicious with fried chicken escalopes licked with mustard or a bavette steak with garlic butter, but here it's made with Savoy cabbage, that tad lighter than the norm of thick strands of white cabbage. A celeriac remoulade is also a great all-rounder, and particularly good with a selection of cheese at lunchtime.

And then there are a couple of little salads that rely on tins of beans. If, however, you come across fresh or semi-dried beans in their pods, such as the French 'coco' or haricot beans, these cook up to creamy tenderness in about twenty minutes. A packet of button mushrooms is also a good staple to pop into the basket on the way round the supermarket. Finely sliced, they make the most delicate of side salads.

Tomatoes would be my desert island vegetable. A plate of sliced tomatoes on the table is as standard in our house as a green salad. And even when it's not called for, it's a very good reason for getting out the cheese afterwards and wiping the plate clean of juices with a crust of bread. Although that in itself can become a bad habit – I hate to think how many calories I've consumed over the years grazing on what amounts to a second dinner.

a gorgeous tomato salad

700g assorted tomatoes, e.g. cherry,
   plum and beefsteak
¾ teaspoon sea salt
½ teaspoon caster sugar
a handful of fresh green or purple basil
   leaves, torn
6 tablespoons extra virgin olive oil

Serves 4

Cherry tomatoes excepted, cut out the core from the tomatoes. Halve, quarter or slice the tomatoes as seems appropriate; a serrated knife is good for this. Arrange on a large plate, sprinkle with the salt and sugar and leave for 30 minutes. Sprinkle with basil and pour over the olive oil.

Crisp rashers of bacon are especially good
with the sweet tartness of the apple, which
in turn is especially good with celeriac, but
vegetarians can turn to dates or some nice
plump prunes as an alternative.

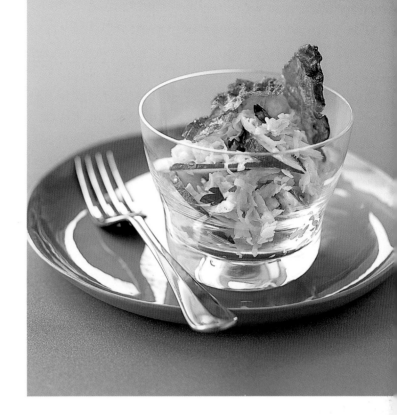

apple and celeriac remoulade

Remoulade

1 celeriac bulb (approx. 800g), peeled

1 level teaspoon sea salt

12 rashers of rindless unsmoked
  streaky bacon

1 red-skinned apple, quartered, cored
  and thinly sliced lengthways

1 tablespoon lemon juice

4 tablespoons coarsely chopped
  fresh flat-leaf parsley, plus a
  little extra to serve

Mayonnaise

1 large organic egg yolk

2 tablespoons Dijon mustard

250ml groundnut oil

1 tablespoon lemon juice

Serves 6

Finely grate the celeriac. Toss it with the sea salt in a large bowl and leave for
20 minutes. Heat the grill, lay the rashers of bacon out on the grid of a grill pan
and cook either side until golden and crisp.

Whisk the egg yolk and mustard together in a bowl, then whisk in the oil, very
slowly to begin with until the mayonnaise takes, then in slightly bolder streams.
Whisk in the lemon juice. It will be a little thinner than a normal mayonnaise.

Place the celeriac in batches in a clean tea towel and wring out as much liquid
as possible – this should rid it of any browning juices. Return it to the bowl and
tease the lumps with your fingers to unravel the strands. Add the mayonnaise and
blend with a wooden spoon. Toss the apple with the lemon juice and mix into the
celeriac with the parsley. Transfer the salad to a clean bowl and scatter with a
little extra parsley.

Serve the remoulade with a slice or two of bacon draped on top. The remoulade
can also be made several hours in advance, in which case cover and chill until
required, bringing it back up to room temperature 30 minutes before serving.

Even though coleslaw is classically made using white cabbage, I prefer Savoy, which is that much more delicate and leafy. But here, as with any coleslaw, fineness is everything, so sharpen up that vegetable knife before setting to.

savoy coleslaw

1 heaped tablespoon sesame seeds

1 Savoy cabbage, tough outer leaves removed

2 teaspoons Dijon mustard

200g soured cream

½ teaspoon caster sugar

sea salt, black pepper

50g currants

3 tablespoons coarsely chopped fresh coriander leaves, plus a little extra to serve

Serves 6

Heat a large frying pan over a medium heat and toast the sesame seeds until golden, stirring occasionally. Transfer them to a bowl and leave to cool.

Quarter the cabbage, remove the core, slice as finely as possible, and place in a large bowl.

To make the dressing, blend the mustard with the soured cream, then add the sugar and some seasoning. Toss the cabbage with the dressing, then mix in the currants and coriander leaves. Transfer to a serving plate or bowl, and scatter over the sesame seeds and a little more coriander. You can prepare the salad up to a couple of hours in advance, in which case cover and set aside in a cool place.

fruit 'n' feta

feta, pomegranate and hazelnut salad

Full of clean, crisp flavours, especially good around Christmas when your palate's dozed off after all the rich seasonal fare.

100g hazelnuts, cut in half
seeds of 3 pomegranates
400g feta, cut into 1cm dice
3 handfuls of fresh flat-leaf
   parsley leaves

4 tablespoons extra virgin olive oil
1 tablespoon lemon juice
black pepper

Serves 6

Preheat the oven to 170°C fan/190°C/gas mark 5. Lay the hazelnuts in a single layer on a small baking tray and toast in the oven for 10 minutes until golden. Remove and leave them to cool.

Put the pomegranate seeds in a bowl and add the feta, hazelnuts and parsley. Pour over the olive oil and lemon juice, and add a grinding of black pepper. Very gently toss to combine the ingredients. You can prepare this salad a couple of hours in advance.

orange, feta and herb salad

Here cubes of feta sit marinating in olive oil and lemon juice before being acquainted with a leafy mass of herbs and juicy orange segments. The ingredients are layered, so you can make it well in advance and toss it at the last minute.

2 oranges
400g feta, cut into 1cm dice
6 tablespoons extra virgin
   olive oil
1½ tablespoons lemon juice
1 red onion, peeled, halved
   and finely sliced

50g mixture of fresh mint,
   coriander and flat-leaf
   parsley leaves

Serves 4

Cut the skin and outer pith off the oranges. Thinly slice them crosswise, then into quarters.

Put the feta in the bottom of a large deep salad bowl and pour over the olive oil and lemon juice. Scatter the onion on top, separating out the strands. Next arrange the herb leaves in a layer, and finally scatter over the orange. Cover with clingfilm and set aside in a cool place until ready to eat.

Just before eating, plunge a couple of spoons into the bottom of the bowl and gently toss the salad, turning it just a few times to avoid breaking the feta up.

Fresh pulses are such a treat, sweet and creamy with none of the dry chalkiness that so often characterises dried pulses. Would they were more readily available here – snap them up should you come across them, and cook them as below.

borlotti bean, red onion and tomato salad

4 plum tomatoes

350g tinned borlotti beans (2 x 300g tins, or 1½ x 400g tins), rinsed*

1 small red onion, peeled, halved and thinly sliced

5 tablespoons coarsely chopped fresh flat-leaf parsley

6 tablespoons extra virgin olive oil

1 tablespoon lemon juice

sea salt, black pepper

Serves 4

Bring a small pan of water to the boil. Cut out a cone from the top of each tomato, plunge them first into the boiling water for 20 seconds, then into cold water. Slip off the skins, quarter, discarding the seeds, then dice the remaining flesh.

Combine the borlotti beans, red onion, diced tomato and parsley in a bowl. Pour over the olive oil and lemon juice and toss, then season to taste with salt and pepper.

*For fresh beans, place in a shallow ovenproof container. Cover with water by 2cm, then add about 5 unpeeled garlic cloves, a sprig of fresh rosemary, a bay leaf and a halved tomato. Pour over 2 tablespoons of olive oil, cover with foil and bake for 1–2 hours at 170°C fan/190°C/gas mark 5 until tender. Leave them to cool in the water.

This is crisp and sharp, a great one for a barbecue line-up, especially if you are cooking crispy chicken wings or thighs. And it's all said and done in five minutes, courtesy of the tinned chickpeas.

rocket, celery and chickpea salad

1 celery heart, trimmed and thinly sliced
1 x 400g tin of chickpeas, rinsed
4 tablespoons extra virgin olive oil
1 tablespoon lemon juice
sea salt, black pepper
50g rocket, coarsely chopped

Serves 4

Combine the celery and chickpeas in a large bowl, and toss with the olive oil, lemon juice and some seasoning. You can prepare the salad to this point in advance, cover and set it aside.

Shortly before eating, toss in the rocket.

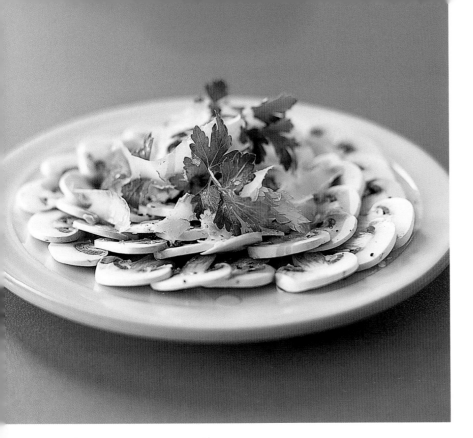

Button mushrooms are delicious eaten raw, sliced wafer thin. If you're after a salad to simply plonk on the table rather than arrange on plates, toss the mushrooms and celery in a large bowl with oil to coat them. Squeeze over a little lemon juice, season and toss again, then mix in the parsley and scatter the Parmesan on top.

button mushroom carpaccio

150g button mushrooms, stalks
    trimmed, finely sliced
1 inner heart of celery, i.e. 2 or
    3 very pale green leafy stalks
extra virgin olive oil
sea salt, black pepper
60g finely sliced Parmesan
2 tablespoons coarsely chopped
    fresh flat-leaf parsley
lemon wedges to serve

Serves 2–4

Either arrange the mushroom slices over two large plates, or four smaller plates if it's intended as a starter, then scatter over the celery. Drizzle over a couple of tablespoons of olive oil and season. Scatter the Parmesan on top, drizzle over a little more oil, then scatter with the parsley and pop a lemon wedge or two on the side of each plate. Serve as soon as possible. The ingredients can also be prepared in advance, and then dressed at the last minute.

This is a good salad for a picnic, when it's nice to have something raw and crunchy. And it's not too hearty – the vegetables are very finely sliced and soften up a touch after a spell in olive oil.

fennel, carrot and radish salad with olives

1 fennel bulb, trimmed and outer
  sheath discarded, halved and
  finely sliced

6 radishes, trimmed and finely sliced

2 slim carrots, trimmed, peeled and
  finely sliced

½ red onion, peeled and finely sliced

100g green and black olives,
  pitted and finely sliced

3 tablespoons extra virgin olive oil

1 teaspoon balsamic vinegar

sea salt, black pepper

Serves 6

Combine all the vegetables and the olives in a shallow dish, and toss with the olive oil and vinegar. Season the salad just before serving – if you do this in advance the salt will draw the juices out of the vegetables and they'll lose their freshness. Cover and leave in a cool place.

Lovers of Russian salad will favour this one, a mixture of broad and green beans in a light tarragon mayonnaise. Some quail's eggs or cooked tail-on prawns would be good in its company.

beans in mayonnaise

350g fine green beans,
   stalk ends trimmed, halved
180g fresh or frozen broad beans
1 organic egg yolk
½ teaspoon Dijon mustard
a squeeze of lemon juice
125ml groundnut oil
sea salt, black pepper
1 teaspoon chopped fresh tarragon

Serves 4–6

Bring two medium pans of salted water to the boil. Add the green beans to one of the pans and cook for 2–3 minutes until just tender, then remove to a sink of cold water to cool. Add the broad beans to the other, and simmer for 3–4 minutes if frozen, 6 minutes if fresh. Drain, leave to cool and then skin them.

Whisk the egg yolk with the mustard and the lemon juice. Gradually whisk in the groundnut oil, then thin with a drop of water, season and add a little chopped tarragon. Toss with the beans.

This Moroccan salad will grace any line-up of mezze, with some dips and warmed mini flat-breads, cocktail gherkins or other pickles and olives. And it's particularly good with feta.

carrot and cumin salad

600g bunched carrots, trimmed, peeled, halved lengthways if large and sliced diagonally

6 tablespoons extra virgin olive oil

1 teaspoon cumin seeds, coarsely ground

1 garlic clove, peeled and crushed to a paste

sea salt

a generous squeeze of lemon juice

a few handfuls of rocket leaves to serve

Serves 6

Bring a medium pan of salted water to the boil, add the carrots and simmer for 5 minutes or until just tender. Drain into a colander or sieve, leave to steam dry for a few minutes, then place in a bowl. Dress with the olive oil, cumin, garlic, some salt and a generous squeeze of lemon juice to taste. Leave to cool. Shortly before serving, toss a pile of rocket leaves into the salad.

green salads

A beautiful green salad is one of the benchmarks of home cooking. For some it is how you poach an egg that reveals the kind of cook you are, whereas for me it is how you toss a pile of green leaves.

That said, it doesn't help that so many salad leaves are now sold in lifeless plastic pouches. Even at their very freshest, to prepare a decent salad with these is never going to be more than a salvage operation. By the time you have cut off the browning edges and cherry-picked the tender leaf from the tough stalk, you would have done better to start with a whole lettuce or head of leaves. Big blowsy escaroles, mop-headed frisées and crisp heads of Romaine are a treat. And in their absence, Little Gem hearts are nearly always available. Those floppy English lettuces that could have been pencil-drawn in a Beatrix Potter sketch are also not to be sniffed at.

You can plump them out with mustard and cress, rocket and watercress, the latter ideally bought by the bunch to guarantee its maturity and sharp peppery savour. Lamb's lettuce or mâche too is at its best bought with its whiskery roots attached and traces of the soil it grew in. Some or any of these make a fine start, with a few slivers of spring onion to spice them up – the selection of these gets better and better, ranging in size from pencil-slim to buxom beauties in shades of purple as well as green.

And so to the dressing. It's worth making up a generous-sized jar of vinaigrette, and having a stock favourite formula that's personal to you. The one that follows has a little bit of everything I like to find in a salad dressing – some Dijon mustard, sugar and a suspicion of garlic, and not too much olive oil, just enough to let its presence be felt. Thick dressings with thin leaves are also particularly alluring – a dollop of green goddess mayo or some homemade salad cream.

This is the kind of green salad that has us coming back for more, though it doesn't have to feature this many types of green leaf. If it's supper for two at home, you may well just want to run to the one type, while the dressing is a great basic and worth adapting to your taste to make up in quantity.

a gorgeous green salad

Dressing

1 tablespoon red wine vinegar
½ teaspoon wholegrain mustard
½ teaspoon Dijon mustard
½ garlic clove, peeled and crushed to
　a paste
1 teaspoon caster sugar
sea salt, black pepper
2 tablespoons extra virgin olive oil
5 tablespoons groundnut oil

Salad

1 Romaine lettuce heart, damaged
　leaves discarded, sliced 1–2cm thick
a handful or two of lamb's lettuce
a handful or two of watercress sprigs
½ punnet of mustard and cress
2 spring onions, thinly sliced

Serves 4

Whisk the vinegar, mustards, garlic, sugar and seasoning in a bowl, then gradually whisk in the oils until you have a light emulsified dressing.

Toss the Romaine lettuce, lamb's lettuce and watercress in a large salad bowl, and scatter the mustard and cress and spring onions in the centre. Toss with the dressing just before serving.

Oh-so pretty, a selection of crisp lettuce hearts and micro leaves. These perfectly formed miniatures consist of the cotyledon (the first two leaves to shoot), and the first true leaves below, and they stop you mid-forkful by dint of their sheer daintiness, they are also beautifully tender. But don't be boxed in by the selection – if you can't find micro leaves, tear some ordinary herbs into pieces. Pea shoots, however, are at last ubiquitous.

lettuce heart and little leaf salad

Dressing

1 medium organic egg yolk
1 teaspoon Dijon mustard
100ml avocado oil, plus 2 tablespoons
a squeeze of lemon juice, plus
   1 tablespoon
sea salt

Salad

2 green Little Gem hearts
1 red Little Gem heart
2 small heads of red chicory
a few pinches of sprouts, e.g. alfalfa
   and radish
a small handful of pea shoots
4 tablespoons fresh micro herbs,
   e.g. basil and coriander
4 breakfast radishes, trimmed and
   finely sliced

Serves 4

Make the dressing close to the time of serving to avoid it separating – it should be the consistency of a thin mayonnaise. Whisk the egg yolk with the mustard in a bowl, then slowly whisk in 100ml of avocado oil a few drops at a time to begin with until the dressing emulsifies. Add a squeeze of lemon juice.

Trim the base of the lettuce hearts and chicory, discarding any damaged outer leaves. Cut the red chicory and red Little Gem heart into quarters or thin segments, and slice the green Little Gem hearts across. Gently toss these in a bowl with 1 tablespoon of lemon juice, 2 tablespoons of avocado oil and a little salt and arrange on a large serving plate. Place a few pinches of sprouts here and there. Drizzle over about two-thirds of the dressing, reserving the rest for some other use. Scatter over the pea shoots, micro herbs and radishes.

The stuff of dreamy delis – flat squeaky-crisp roasted Marcona almonds, juicy muscatel raisins on the vine, and ewe's or goat's milk cheese just beginning to ooze below the rind. In fact Little Gems have never seemed more glam.

little gem, almond and raisin salad with wigmore

2 Little Gem hearts, trimmed
  and leaves separated
150g thin slices of soft or semi-soft
  ewe's or goat's milk cheese, e.g.
  Wigmore, Capricorn, Kidderton Ash
rapeseed or extra virgin olive oil
a squeeze of lemon juice
a pinch of sea salt
50g roasted, salted Marcona almonds
50g muscatel raisins
2 spring onions, trimmed
  and thinly sliced

Serves 4

Arrange the leaves from the Little Gem hearts on a large plate with the cheese. Drizzle over some oil, squeeze over a little lemon juice and season with a pinch of salt, then scatter over the almonds, raisins and spring onions.

The French, with astute rationale, serve cheese before the pudding, hence avoiding the confusion of going from savoury to sweet and back again, which wreaks havoc with the wines. But more than this, a small salad with the cheese course does away with filling up on biscuits at a stage of the meal when the last thing you feel like is another dose of carbs. The dressing is that little bit tarter than most vinaigrettes, which usually contain a generous hit of sugar to soothe the vinegar.

green salad for cheese

Salad
salad leaves for 6 small green salads,
   e.g. escarole, lamb's lettuce, Little
   Gem leaves, or a mixture

Dressing
2 teaspoons sherry vinegar
a squeeze of lemon juice
½ teaspoon Dijon mustard
sea salt, black pepper
1 teaspoon finely chopped shallot
½ garlic clove, peeled, finely chopped
3 tablespoons extra virgin olive oil

Serves 6

Whisk the vinegar and lemon juice with the mustard and seasoning in a bowl. Add the shallot and garlic and the oil.

Just before serving toss the leaves with the dressing in a bowl.

This salad is mainly an excuse to eat a large plate of very fine smoked salmon, with the cucumber fromage frais a civilised intermediary between the two.

peppery salad with cucumber fromage frais

1 cucumber

sea salt

½ teaspoon caster sugar

150g fromage frais

juice of ¼ lemon

3 spring onions, trimmed and finely sliced

400g smoked salmon (optional)

black pepper

mixture of rocket, watercress, and mustard
   and cress, to feed 4

groundnut oil

Serves 4

Trim the ends off the cucumber and peel it. Quarter it lengthways and cut out the seeds. Cut each quarter into thin strips, then slice these into 2–3cm lengths. Place the cucumber in a bowl and toss with ½ teaspoon of salt and the sugar. Leave for 30 minutes to exude its juices, then drain in a sieve, rinse thoroughly under the cold tap and pat dry on a tea towel. Mix the cucumber in a bowl with the fromage frais, a squeeze of lemon juice, and half the spring onion.

Lay out the smoked salmon (if using) on four plates and grind over a little black pepper. Toss the leaves in a bowl with enough oil to coat, then add a few drops of lemon juice and the smallest pinch of sea salt. Place a pile of leaves on the plates, with a pile of cucumber salad. Scatter over the remaining spring onion.

My green credentials desert me when it comes to green beans – in the dark, snowy depths of winter, wafer-fine beans are that little bit too hard to resist even though they do come from the other side of the world.

chunky green salad

200g fine green beans,
  stalk ends trimmed
1 medium courgette (approx. 200g),
  trimmed and very finely sliced
¼ red onion, finely sliced
juice of 1 lemon
extra virgin olive oil
sea salt, black pepper
2 avocados (ideally Hass)
2 punnets of mustard and cress
50g finely sliced Parmesan

Serves 4

Bring a large pan of salted water to the boil and cook the beans for 3–4 minutes until just tender. Transfer to a sink of cold water, using a slotted spoon. Once cool, remove and drain on a tea-towel.

Toss the courgette, beans and red onion in a salad bowl with the lemon juice, 3 tablespoons of olive oil and some seasoning. Quarter the avocados and remove the stone, then peel off the skin and cut into long thin slices. Carefully fold these into the salad, then gently toss in the mustard and cress. Pile on to plates, scatter over the Parmesan and pour over a little more oil.

We've cut out the guilty bits here – the eggs and Parmesan – and baked the croutons for a lighter Caesar. But given that anchovies never went terribly well with cheese in the first place, it's no bad thing. Though you can always serve Parmesan on the side for those who can't live without it.

caesar salad 'lite'

4 thin slices of sourdough bread, crusts
   removed, cut to approx. 1cm dice
8 tablespoons extra virgin olive oil
½ teaspoon dried oregano
sea salt, black pepper
1 tablespoon lemon juice
1 teaspoon Worcestershire sauce
1 small garlic clove, peeled
   and crushed
2 Romaine hearts
2 avocados (ideally Hass)
6 salted anchovy fillets, halved
   lengthways
3 tablespoons snipped fresh chives

Serves 4–6

Preheat the oven to 180°C fan/200°C/gas mark 6. Toss the bread cubes with 1 tablespoon of olive oil, the oregano and a pinch of salt. Scatter them over a baking sheet and toast in the oven for 9–11 minutes until light gold. Leave to cool.

To make the dressing, whisk the lemon juice, Worcestershire sauce, garlic and some seasoning in a small bowl, then whisk in the remaining oil.

Separate out the leaves from the lettuces and cut them into chunky pieces. Quarter the avocados and remove the stone, then peel off the skin and cut into long thin slices. Combine the lettuce, avocado, anchovies and chives in a large shallow dish or bowl. Pour over the dressing and scatter over the croutons.

Frisée lettuces can vary hugely in size, so if it's an enormous blowsy affair use enough leaves for four and reserve the remainder for another salad. Dark green and tough outside leaves needn't go to waste – they're a delight wilted in olive oil with a little garlic and chilli, their bitterness receding into the distance as they are heated.

very norman market day

Salad

1 frisée lettuce

120g fine green beans, stalk ends trimmed and halved

6 large cherry tomatoes, cut into wedges

175g lardons, or diced rindless unsmoked streaky bacon

2 thick slices of pain de Campagne or coarse-textured white bread, cut into 1–2cm dice

Dressing

1 tablespoon Dijon mustard

2 teaspoons red wine vinegar

sea salt

3 tablespoons groundnut oil

Serves 4

The best way to prepare a frisée lettuce is to hold it by the stalk and give it a radical trim around the edges, removing several inches of the dark green leaves at the top which are tough and bitter to eat. Now cut out the stalk and discard the periphery of outer leaves. Separate and tear up the remaining pale green fronds and wash them in a sink of cold water. Shake or spin them dry and place them in a large salad bowl. Bring a small pan of salted water to the boil, add the beans and simmer for 3–4 minutes, leaving them firm to the bite. Drain and refresh them in cold water, then toss them into the leaves with the tomatoes.

To make the dressing, whisk the mustard with the vinegar and some sea salt in a small bowl, then whisk in the oil.

Heat a frying pan over a medium-low heat and fry the lardons for about 4 minutes, stirring occasionally. Add the bread to the pan and continue to cook for another 4 minutes, tossing frequently, until the lardons are frazzled and crisp and the bread has started to toast at the edges. Toss the salad with the dressing. Distribute the contents of the pan over the top of the salad, toss it, and serve straight away, while the lardons and croutons are warm.

The heartstone here is those quintessential English salad ingredients that we love to smother in salad cream – boiled eggs, floppy green lettuce leaves, radishes and spring onions. If you have the English country garden to eat it in, so much the better.

english country garden salad

Salad Cream

3 medium egg yolks
4 tablespoons double cream
1 teaspoon English mustard
1 teaspoon caster sugar
1 tablespoon white wine vinegar
sea salt

Salad

12 quail's eggs
2 floppy green lettuces
2 handfuls long radishes, trimmed
4 spring onions, trimmed and thinly
   sliced diagonally
2 tablespoons coarsely snipped
   fresh chives

Serves 6

Whisk all the ingredients for the salad cream in a bowl set over a pan with a little simmering water in it, then stir constantly for a few minutes until it thickens, taking care not to overheat it otherwise it will scramble. Pass the salad cream through a sieve into a bowl, cover the surface with clingfilm, leave to cool, then chill until required.

Bring a small pan of water to the boil and carefully lower in the quail's eggs. Cook for 2½ minutes, then drain, refill the pan with cold water and leave to cool. Shell the eggs by pinching a little of the shell and gently pulling to remove it.

Twist the base off the lettuces, discard the leathery outer leaves, and without separating the remainder rinse the lettuce under the cold tap inside and out. Thoroughly shake the lettuces dry and then place each one in a bowl, opening out the leaves as though they were a flower. Scatter over the radishes, spring onions and eggs. The salads can be prepared to this point in advance, in which case cover and set aside.

Just before serving, spoon the salad cream over the salads and scatter over the chives.

White balsamic vinegar is a relative newcomer on the block, and altogether different from the dark kind. It's delicate, sweet and sour, and great in salads that call for a little sharpening without the full-on acidity of a wine vinegar. Avocado oil too is relatively new, but seems here to stay, and has a real taste of the fruit itself. But as ever, oils and vinegars are open to whatever largesse your cupboard is offering up.

salad of baby spinach, avocado and dates

1 tablespoon white balsamic vinegar

sea salt, black pepper

4 tablespoons avocado oil

150g Greek-style yoghurt

a pinch of saffron filaments (about 20), ground and infused with 1 teaspoon boiling water

2 avocados (ideally Hass)

150g baby spinach

150g Medjool dates, stoned and cut into long thin strips

30g walnut pieces

Serves 4–6

Whisk the vinegar with some seasoning in a bowl, then whisk in the oil. Blend the yoghurt with the saffron infusion and a little salt in another bowl. The two dressings can be prepared in advance, in which case cover and chill the yoghurt.

Quarter the avocados and remove from the stone, then peel off the skin and cut the flesh into long thin strips. Toss the spinach leaves with the vinaigrette in a large bowl or shallow serving dish, then mix in the avocado and dates. Scatter over the walnuts, and serve as soon as possible with the bowl of yoghurt on the side.

lovely rich dressings

These lie the other side of the fence from vinaigrettes, thick and unctuous, for dolloping on chunky Cos, Romaine and Little Gem leaves, though there's nothing to stop you dressing them with a vinaigrette first. Some will also serve as a little sauce for grilled meat or fish, and are good for dipping too.

green goddess mayo

This belongs to the Martini era. Slather it over halves of boiled egg, dish it up with a bowl of lightly cooked quail's eggs, or spread it over warm blinis with some smoked salmon, or salmon roe and snipped chives.

150g Hellmann's mayonnaise
1 spring onion, trimmed and chopped
2 tablespoons chopped fresh coriander leaves
2 tablespoons chopped fresh basil leaves
1 teaspoon chopped fresh tarragon leaves

Serves 4

Place all the ingredients in the bowl of a food processor and whiz to a green sauce. Transfer to a bowl, cover and chill until required.

easy salad cream

Quicker than the real thing (see page 183), this is basically Heinz with a little bit of help. For a simple salad arrange four trimmed and quartered Little Gem lettuces on four plates, with a few trimmed radishes and a halved spring onion on each, and drizzle the dressing over.

3 tablespoons Heinz salad cream
3 tablespoons single cream or low-fat yoghurt
½ teaspoon English mustard

Serves 4

Blend together all the ingredients for the salad cream in a bowl, cover and chill until required.

garlic yoghurt dressing

Creamy but not overly rich, dollop this over Romaine or Cos leaves and scatter with slivers of green or purple spring onions.

200g creamy yoghurt
pinch of caster sugar
sea salt
1 garlic clove, peeled and crushed to a paste
2 tablespoons extra virgin olive oil

Serves 4–6

Blend all the ingredients for the dressing together in a bowl. You can make this well in advance, in which case cover and chill it.

devilled english dressing

This gorgeous sunny yellow dressing sports wholly English credentials, being made with rapeseed oil. It's a green option for all those who want to cook and eat ingredients produced close to home.

1 tablespoon cider vinegar
2 teaspoons Colman's English mustard
1 scant teaspoon caster sugar
sea salt
7 tablespoons rapeseed oil

Serves 4

Whisk the vinegar, mustard, sugar and a little salt together in a medium bowl, then gradually whisk in the oil a tablespoon or two at a time until the dressing emulsifies – it should by the end be thick, unctuous and dark yellow. If necessary give it another whisk before using, to emulsify it again.

walnut and garlic dressing

This feisty Balkan dressing is good cold-weather stuff as well as hot, and you could serve it with some cooked veggies or cold roast chicken, and salad leaves.

1 slice of white bread, crusts removed
1 garlic clove, peeled
50g shelled walnuts
2 tablespoons walnut oil
a squeeze of lemon juice
½ teaspoon sea salt
½ teaspoon caster sugar
3 heaped tablespoons Greek yoghurt

Serves 4

Briefly soak the bread in water and then squeeze it out using your hands. Whiz together the garlic clove, walnuts, bread, walnut oil, lemon juice, sea salt and sugar. Add the Greek yoghurt and blend. Cover and chill until required.

index

acknowledgements

With many thanks to Angela Mason, to my agent Rosemary Sandberg, to Suzanna de Jong, Editor, Annie Lee, Copy Editor, and to Kyle Cathie. And with love and thanks to Jonnie, Rothko and Louis.